5 STEPS TO A 5™

500 AP Psychology Questions to know by test day

Also in the 5 Steps Series:
5 Steps to a 5: AP Psychology
5 Steps to a 5: AP Psychology with CD-ROM
5 Steps to a 5: AP Psychology Flashcards for Your iPod
5 Steps to a 5: AP Psychology (iPhone App)

Also in the 500 AP Questions to Know by Test Day series:
5 Steps to a 5: 500 AP English Language Questions to Know by Test Day
5 Steps to a 5: 500 AP English Literature Questions to Know by Test Day
5 Steps to a 5: 500 AP Biology Questions to Know by Test Day
5 Steps to a 5: 500 AP U.S. History Questions to Know by Test Day
5 Steps to a 5: 500 AP World History Questions to Know by Test Day

500 AP Psychology Questions to know by test day

Lauren Williams

New York Chicago San Francisco Athens London Madrid
Mexico City Milan New Delhi Singapore Sydney Toronto

LAUREN WILLIAMS has a bachelor's degree in history and psychology and a master's degree in social studies education. She has been a teacher in New York City for 12 years, having taught advanced placement psychology for nine years. She is currently working toward a second master's degree in counseling.

8 9 10 11 12 13 14 15 FGR/FGR 0 1 9 8 7 6

ISBN 978-0-07-174203-0
MHID 0-07-174203-4

e-ISBN 978-0-07-174204-7
e-MHID 0-07-174204-2

Library of Congress Control Number 2010935998

Series interior design by Jane Tenenbaum

This book is printed on acid-free paper.

CONTENTS

INTRODUCTION

Congratulations! You've taken a big step toward AP success by purchasing *5 Steps to a 5: 500 AP Psychology Questions to Know by Test Day*. We are here to help you take the next step and score high on your AP Exam so you can earn college credits and get into the college or university of your choice.

This book gives you 500 AP-style multiple-choice questions that cover all the most essential course material. Each question has a detailed answer explanation. These questions will give you valuable independent practice to supplement your regular textbook and the groundwork you are already doing in your AP classroom.

This and the other books in this series were written by expert AP teachers who know your exam inside out and can identify the crucial exam information as well as questions that are most likely to appear on the exam.

You might be the kind of student who takes several AP courses and needs to study extra questions a few weeks before the exam for a final review. Or you might be the kind of student who puts off preparing until the last weeks before the exam. No matter what your preparation style is, you will surely benefit from reviewing these 500 questions, which closely parallel the content, format, and degree of difficulty of the questions on the actual AP exam. These questions and their answer explanations are the ideal last-minute study tool for those final few weeks before the test.

Remember the old saying "Practice makes perfect." If you practice with all the questions and answers in this book, we are certain you will build the skills and confidence needed to do great on the exam. Good luck!

—Editors of McGraw-Hill Education

CHAPTER 1

Schools of Thought

1. Jill wants to study the process of thinking. Which field of psychology should she choose?

(A) Cognitive
(B) Social
(C) Personality
(D) Learning
(E) Perception

2. I believe people choose to live meaningful lives. I share many of the same beliefs as Carl Rogers. Most important, I believe many people have the ability to reach self-actualization. Who am I?

(A) Wertheimer
(B) Skinner
(C) Maslow
(D) Terman
(E) Seligman

3. Of the following, who is associated with the Gestalt school of psychology?

(A) John Watson
(B) William James
(C) Ivan Pavlov
(D) Max Wertheimer
(E) Sigmund Freud

4. Which of the following psychologists wrote *The Principles of Psychology*?

(A) William James
(B) Wilhelm Wundt
(C) John Watson
(D) Sigmund Freud
(E) Max Wertheimer

5. Psychology is considered a science mainly because it relies on direct observation. Which field of psychology supports this?

(A) Behaviorism
(B) Psychodynamic psychology
(C) Social psychology
(D) Cognitive psychology
(E) Structuralism

6. Which of the following best defines eclectic psychology?

(A) The study of animal instinct
(B) The study of child development
(C) The study of abnormal behavior
(D) The study of a variety of theories within the field
(E) The study of the human brain and central nervous system

7. Psychoanalytic psychology focuses mainly on:

(A) Rewards and punishments
(B) Self-esteem and self-actualization
(C) Biology and genetics
(D) Internal conflict and unconscious desires
(E) Sensation and perception

8. One major criticism of Ivan Pavlov's concept of classical conditioning was that:

(A) It did not take into account voluntary human behavior.
(B) It was unethical to use dogs in a psychology experiment.
(C) It did not take into account involuntary behavior.
(D) The findings overlapped with other fields of psychology.
(E) It did not relate to human behavior.

9. Which of the following psychologists was a structuralist?

(A) John Watson
(B) Wilhelm Wundt
(C) William James
(D) Max Wertheimer
(E) Sigmund Freud

10. The use of rewards, punishments, and positive reinforcement is an example of which field of psychology?

(A) Personality
(B) Behavioral
(C) Social
(D) Cognitive
(E) Psychoanalytic

11. "Give me a dozen healthy infants and my own special world to bring them up in, and I'll guarantee to take any one at random and train him to become any type of specialist, . . . lawyer, doctor . . ." What psychological approach would support this statement?

(A) Cognitive
(B) Structural
(C) Functional
(D) Behavioral
(E) Psychoanalytic

12. Who was considered the father of psychology?

(A) James
(B) Wundt
(C) Wertheimer
(D) Freud
(E) Kohler

13. One major difference between structuralism and functionalism is:

(A) Structuralists analyze all mental elements, while functionalists analyze only some elements.
(B) Structuralists believe all behaviors stem from the evolutionary process.
(C) Structuralists wish to divide the mind into mental elements while functionalists believe behavior helps an organism adapt to the environment.
(D) Only functionalists believe in the importance of introspection.
(E) Structuralists try to manipulate the mind in order to understand behavior, while functionalists study the conscious mind to understand behavior.

14. The idea that psychology is not based on scientific fact or human shortcomings but instead should focus on human experience is the basis for which psychological approach?

(A) Cognitive psychology
(B) Structuralism
(C) Behaviorism
(D) Functionalism
(E) Humanism

15. Clients who work with their therapists to explore their past to discover the source of their illness would be seeking what type of therapy?

(A) Psychoanalytic
(B) Humanist
(C) Cognitive
(D) Eclectic
(E) Behavioral

16. Psychodynamic psychology focuses mainly on which of the following?

(A) Free will and self-actualization
(B) Experiments in controlled settings
(C) The collective unconscious
(D) Thoughts, impulses, and desires beyond the conscious being
(E) Practical introspection

17. A developmental psychologist focuses mainly on:

(A) The conscious experiences of an infant
(B) The manner in which a child develops the ability to speak, learn, and understand the world around him or her
(C) The mental process that helps a young person adapt to his or her environment
(D) The identification of one's environment and response to the environment
(E) Experiments that emphasize actual behavior, rather than controlled settings

18. Phenomenology is best defined as:

(A) The study of natural, unanalyzed perception
(B) The process of thinking and memory
(C) The study of psychological mental health
(D) The study of language development
(E) The process of consistent patterns and organized sets

19. The term *biological psychology* is concerned with:

(A) Aggression and sexual behavior
(B) Depression and anxiety
(C) Genetics and the nervous system
(D) Social anxiety
(E) Drug treatment

20. A case study is:

(A) A primary tool for investigation into a client's unconscious through dream analysis and free association
(B) A study done over an entire life span of one individual, giving the psychologist detailed information of one's psyche
(C) A study that exposes the subject to some event and measures coping skills
(D) An independent study used outside the natural environment of the subject
(E) A comparative study of various people of different ages at the same time

CHAPTER 2

Research Methods

21. Which of the following research methods does not permit researchers to draw conclusions regarding cause-and-effect relationships?

(A) Experimental research
(B) Surveys
(C) Case studies
(D) Correlational research
(E) Naturalistic observations

22. A random sample can best be defined as:

(A) A sample in which each potential participant has an equal chance of being selected
(B) A sample that is carefully chosen so the characteristics of participants correspond to the larger population
(C) A selection of cases from a larger population
(D) A selection of cases from the control group
(E) A sample of a larger population from the experimental group

23. The Hawthorne effect is best defined as:

(A) Expectations by the experimenter that can influence the results of an experiment
(B) The change in the results of an experiment when it is "blind" versus "double blind"
(C) The idea that people will alter their behavior because of the researchers' attention and not because of actual treatment
(D) Specific, testable predictions derived from a theory
(E) The idea that subjects in an experiment will lie if the researcher tells them to

24. Dr. Bisell conducts an experiment to see whether hunger makes mice run faster through a maze. He randomly assigns 25 mice to a control group or an experimental group. Which cannot be a confounding variable?

(A) Where the experiment takes place
(B) How hungry the mice were before the experiment
(C) How fast the mice are before the race
(D) When the experiment takes place
(E) The population from which he selected the mice

25. Marc, a psychology major, collected survey data about the number of hours that college students study for finals and their grades on those finals. His data indicates that students who spend more time studying for finals tend to do better than other students. What can Marc now conclude?

(A) Studying improves a student's grade on a final exam.
(B) A relationship exists between studying and exam grades.
(C) A significant relationship exists between studying and grades.
(D) Students who do not study for final exams will not do well on those exams.
(E) Students with higher IQs tend to study more than those with lower IQs.

26. Jordan runs an experiment testing the effects of sugar consumption on aggression levels in children. He randomly assigns 20 subjects either to a control group given sugar-free candy or to the experimental group that was given the same candy that did contain sugar. He then tests the subjects' response to several different puzzles, each with increasing difficulty. Jordan hypothesizes that sugar levels do play a role in aggression in children. In order to know whether his hypothesis has been supported, Jordan will need to use:

(A) Descriptive statistics
(B) Means-to-end statistics
(C) Experimental research
(D) Scatter plots
(E) Inferential statistics

27. Which of the following coefficients of a correlation indicate the weakest relationship between two variables?

(A) 0.51
(B) −0.28
(C) 0.08
(D) −1.00
(E) 1.00

28. The observation in a classroom that the higher the room temperature, the lower student performance would be an example of:

(A) Negative correlation
(B) Zero correlation
(C) Positive correlation
(D) Independent correlation
(E) Dependent correlation

29. In an experiment, Sydney is going to investigate how alcohol affects aggression. The number of alcoholic drinks the subject has is called:

(A) Controlled variable
(B) Independent variable
(C) Dependent variable
(D) Experimental variable
(E) Positive variable

30. If a researcher is trying to establish a causal relationship between eating breakfast and work performance, the researcher should use which of the following methods of research?

(A) Case study
(B) Correlational research
(C) Experimental research
(D) Survey
(E) Statistics

CHAPTER 3

The Brain

31. Which part of the brain is responsible for combining sounds into words and arranging words into meaningful sentences?

(A) Broca's area
(B) Wernicke's area
(C) Hypothalamus
(D) Hippocampus
(E) Medulla

32. Damage to the cerebellum would most likely result in:

(A) Respiratory failure
(B) Heart failure
(C) Loss of muscular coordination
(D) Loss of hearing
(E) Loss of memory

33. The pons is located between the medulla and other brain areas. It is responsible for which of the following?

(A) Motor coordination
(B) Seeing and hearing
(C) Sleep and arousal
(D) Balance
(E) Emotional reactions

34. When humans suffer damage to this part of the brain, there can be a lapse into a permanent state of unconsciousness.

(A) Temporal lobe
(B) Parietal lobe
(C) Frontal lobe
(D) Cerebrum
(E) Reticular formation

35. An EEG records:

(A) Direct electrical stimulation of the brain
(B) The number of neurons in the brain
(C) Electrical impulses from the brain
(D) Chemical activity in specific areas of the brain
(E) Stimulation of the frontal lobe

36. Which part of the brain is affected during a split-brain operation?

(A) Cerebellum
(B) Corpus callosum
(C) Cerebrum
(D) Medulla
(E) Pons

37. The limbic system is responsible for

(A) The control of hunger, thirst, and sex
(B) Breathing regulations
(C) Balance and coordination
(D) Speech
(E) Language

38. The main job of the thalamus is:

(A) Receiving sensory information and relaying it to the appropriate area
(B) Processing sensory information about touch, pain, and temperature
(C) Regulating motivational and emotional behavior
(D) Coordinating movements and timed motor responses
(E) Controlling all auditory functions of the brain

39. Bodily sensations such as touch, pressure, and temperature are controlled in which area of the brain?

(A) Occipital lobe
(B) Temporal lobe
(C) Frontal lobe
(D) Parietal lobe
(E) Motor lobe

40. As a result of her car accident, Mimi suffered damage to her Broca's area of the brain. What symptoms will she suffer as a result?

(A) Inability to see color
(B) Inability to speak in fluent sentences
(C) Inability to walk
(D) Inability to remember short term
(E) Inability to remember long term

41. If damage occurs to the occipital lobe, an individual could fail to recognize some objects, persons, or color. This damage is called:

(A) Visual aphasia
(B) Visual agnosia
(C) Neglect syndrome
(D) Occipital agnosia
(E) Temporal aphasia

42. A "split-brain" patient is asked to stare at a black dot between the HE and ART as the word HEART is displayed on a screen. When asked what she sees, what will the patient do?

(A) The patient will say she sees the word HE.
(B) The patient will say she sees the word ART.
(C) The patient will point to the word ART.
(D) The patient will say the word HEART.
(E) The patient will only see a black dot.

43. Knowing what you are touching or how hot to make the water for your shower involves which of these areas of the brain?

(A) Temporal lobe
(B) Motor cortex
(C) Cerebrum
(D) Frontal lobe
(E) Somatosensory cortex

44. Emma is telling her younger sister stories about her first Christmas in their new home. Which part of the brain is Emma using to recall these memories?

(A) Hypothalamus
(B) Thalamus
(C) Amygdala
(D) Hippocampus
(E) Medulla

45. An MRI involves:

(A) Passing nonharmful radio frequencies through the brain to study brain structure
(B) Injecting a slightly radioactive solution into the bloodstream to measure the amount absorbed by the brain
(C) Mapping the brain's activity by having the patient complete cognitive tasks
(D) Following brain images to get an exact measurement of brain size, capacity, and abilities
(E) Testing patients' brain damage after severe brain injuries

46. Maddie is walking down a dark alley by herself late at night. She automatically turns her head to the left when she hears a strange noise. What part of the brain is she using?

(A) Hindbrain
(B) Midbrain
(C) Forebrain
(D) Somatosensory cortex
(E) Motor cortex

47. Dylan has recovered from extensive injury to his left cerebral hemisphere and has continued his career. His occupation is most likely:

(A) Accountant
(B) English teacher
(C) Journalist
(D) Lawyer
(E) Graphic artist

48. Which of the following is *not* controlled by the hypothalamus?

(A) Sex
(B) Eating and drinking
(C) Balance and coordination
(D) Motivation
(E) Emotion

49. Which of the following is *not* part of the limbic system?

(A) Hypothalamus
(B) Thalamus
(C) Cerebellum
(D) Amygdala
(E) Hippocampus

50. Wernicke's area is located on which lobe of the brain?

(A) Left temporal lobe
(B) Right temporal lobe
(C) Left occipital lobe
(D) Right occipital lobe
(E) Left frontal lobe

CHAPTER 4

Neuroscience

51. Which part of the neuron serves as the protective coating?
(A) Axon
(B) Dendrite
(C) Synapse
(D) Myelin sheath
(E) Cell body

52. Another name for the cell body of the neuron is:
(A) Dendrite
(B) Myelin
(C) Soma
(D) Axon
(E) Synaptic vesicle

53. The process by which a tiny electrical current is generated when the positive sodium ions rush inside the axon, causing the inside of the axon to reverse its charge, is called:
(A) Action potential
(B) Ion potential
(C) Resting state
(D) Synaptic state
(E) Negative potential

54. If Mia stepped on a nail, which of the following would be the correct order of communication for her to feel the pain?
(A) Stimulus-electrical impulse-neurotransmitter-receptor site
(B) Electrical impulse-stimulus-receptor site-neurotransmitter
(C) Receptor site-neurotransmitter-electrical impulse-stimulus
(D) Electrical impulse-receptor site-stimulus-neurotransmitter
(E) Stimulus-electrical impulse-receptor site-neurotransmitter

55. What is the job of the sodium pump?

(A) It separates positive ions and places them all inside the axon.
(B) It is responsible for keeping the axon charged by returning and keeping sodium ions outside the axon membrane.
(C) It generates an electrical current when the positive ions rush into the axon.
(D) It generates an electrical current when the negative ions rush into the axon.
(E) It is a neural impulse that transfers negative ions into the neuron.

56. If an action potential starts at the beginning of an axon, the action potential will continue at the same speed to the very end of the axon. This concept is known as:

(A) Nerve impulse
(B) Synapse
(C) Resting state
(D) All-or-none law
(E) Sodium pump

57. Which of the following functions best explains the role of the sympathetic nervous system?

(A) Preparing the body for a traumatic event
(B) Returning the body to equilibrium
(C) Preparing the body for "fight or flight"
(D) Maintaining the body's vital functions
(E) Maintaining homeostasis

58. Which of the following neurotransmitters most closely resembles the affects alcohol has on the nervous system?

(A) Anandamide
(B) GABA
(C) Dopamine
(D) Acetylcholine
(E) Serotonin

59. What is one major difference between the sympathetic and parasympathetic nervous systems?

(A) The sympathetic nervous system increases physiological arousal, while the parasympathetic nervous system returns the body to a calmer and relaxed state.
(B) The sympathetic nervous system is a subdivision of the somatic nervous system, while the parasympathetic nervous system is a subdivision of the autonomic nervous system.
(C) The sympathetic nervous system plays a role in traumatic events, while the parasympathetic nervous system only plays a role in digestion.
(D) The parasympathetic nervous system is used more often than the sympathetic nervous system.
(E) The sympathetic nervous system plays a role in sexual behavior, while the parasympathetic nervous system does not.

60. Neurons that carry information away from the spinal cord to produce responses in various muscles or organs throughout the body are called:

(A) Afferent neurons
(B) Interneurons
(C) Neurotransmitters
(D) Sensor neurons
(E) Efferent neurons

CHAPTER 5

Sensation and Perception

61. The basic experience of the stimulation of the body's senses is called:

(A) Sensation
(B) Perception
(C) Adaptation
(D) Cognition
(E) Conduction

62. Taste: 1 gram of table salt in 500 liters of water; smell: 1 drop of perfume diffused throughout a three-room apartment; touch: the wing of a bee falling on your cheek from a height of 1 centimeter away. These are all examples of:

(A) The just-noticeable difference of our senses
(B) The difference threshold for our senses
(C) The absolute threshold of our senses
(D) The adaptation of our senses
(E) The perception of our senses

63. Weber's law can best be defined as:

(A) The smallest change in stimulation that can be detected 50 percent of the time
(B) The principle that the just-noticeable difference for any given sense is a constant proportion of the stimulation being judged
(C) The principle that there is an adjustment of sensation levels depending on the stimulation received
(D) The idea that the least amount of energy detected in a stimulation only occurs 50 percent of the time
(E) The theory that all stimuli respond to the same sensations through the process of creating meaningful patterns

64. The name of the transparent protective coating over the front part of the eye is:

(A) Lens
(B) Iris
(C) Pupil
(D) Fovea
(E) Cornea

65. The function of the lens is to:

(A) Project an image onto the cornea
(B) Focus an image on the retina
(C) Locate an image
(D) Contain receptor cells that are sensitive to light
(E) Locate the blind spot

66. The greatest density of cones exists in which part of the eye?

(A) Cornea
(B) Lens
(C) Pupil
(D) Fovea
(E) Retina

67. An afterimage can best be defined as:

(A) Sense experience that occurs after a visual stimulus has been removed
(B) Decreased sensitivity of rods and cones in bright light
(C) Increased sensitivity of rods and cones in darkness
(D) Distinguishable fine details of a stimulation
(E) Nondistinguishable details of a stimulation

68. The theory of color that best explains color afterimage is:

(A) The volley theory
(B) The trichromatic theory
(C) The opponent-process theory
(D) The subtractive color theory
(E) The monochromatic theory

69. Trichromats can mix which three colors to perceive virtually any hue?

(A) Red, blue, green
(B) Red, blue, yellow
(C) Blue, yellow, green
(D) Red, green, yellow
(E) Yellow, orange, green

70. The three small bones of the inner ear are called what?

(A) Cochlear bones
(B) Tympanic bones
(C) Basilar
(D) Ossicles
(E) Auditory canals

71. When the molecules of a skunk's spray enter your nose, the molecules are transformed into electrical signals, or impulses, that are interpreted by the brain as an unpleasant odor. This is an example of:

(A) Adaptation
(B) Transduction
(C) Sensation
(D) Perception
(E) Stimulation

72. Which of the following occupations relies heavily on kinesthetic and vestibular senses?

(A) Doctor
(B) Pilot
(C) Gymnast
(D) Artist
(E) Engineer

73. Frequency is to ________________ as amplitude is to ________________.

(A) sensation; perception
(B) loudness; pitch
(C) pitch; loudness
(D) perception; sensation
(E) warmth; cold

74. Olfactory cells are the receptors for what sense?

(A) Taste
(B) Hearing
(C) Vision
(D) Smell
(E) Touch

75. The binocular cue for depth perception based on signals from muscles that turn the eyes to focus on near or approaching objects is called:

(A) Convergence
(B) Retinal disparity
(C) Shape constancy
(D) Interposition
(E) Perceptual vision

76. As a car drives away, it projects a smaller and smaller image on your retina. Although the retinal image grows smaller, you do not perceive the car as shrinking because of:

(A) Shape constancy
(B) Size continuity
(C) Size constancy
(D) Shape continuity
(E) Size perception

77. Which of the following is *not* a monocular depth cue?

(A) Linear perspective
(B) Interposition
(C) Relative size
(D) Texture gradient
(E) Convergence

78. The final step required to convert vibrations into sound sensations takes place in which part of the ear?

(A) Ossicles
(B) Outer ear
(C) Cochlea
(D) Middle ear
(E) Auditory receptors

79. Which of the following statements best defines the gate control theory of pain?

(A) Pain impulses are sent to receptor sites in vital organs.
(B) Nonpainful nerve impulses compete with pain impulses to reach the brain, creating a neural blockage.
(C) Stimuli of various kinds activate free nerve endings.
(D) Pain is simply a psychological state, not a physiological one.
(E) Perception of pain depends on one's physical makeup.

80. Black-and-white vision with greatest sensitivity under low levels of illumination describes the role of:

(A) The cones
(B) The cornea
(C) The fovea
(D) The rods
(E) The pupil

CHAPTER 6

Consciousness, Sleep, and Dreams

81. Which of the following is *not* considered to be an altered state of consciousness?

(A) Sleep
(B) Hypnosis
(C) Psychoactive drugs
(D) Exercise
(E) Meditation

82. Driving a car along a familiar route while listening to the radio or thinking of something else is an example of:

(A) Automatic process
(B) Controlled process
(C) Somatic process
(D) Sympathetic process
(E) Parasympathetic process

83. When researchers removed all time cues, such as light, clock, radio, and television, from subjects' environment, the length of the day expanded from 24 to about 25 hours. This phenomenon is known as:

(A) The interval timing clock
(B) The circadian rhythm
(C) The biological clock
(D) The internal rhythm
(E) The external clock

84. The hormone most closely related to one's sleep patterns is:

(A) Serotonin
(B) Norepinephrine
(C) Epinephrine
(D) Melatonin
(E) Dopamine

85. The sleep stage that is a transition from wakefulness to sleep and lasting 1–7 minutes is:

(A) REM sleep
(B) Stage 1 sleep
(C) Stage 2 sleep
(D) Stage 3 sleep
(E) Stage 4 sleep

86. Which stage of sleep is characterized by delta waves (very high amplitude and very low frequency)?

(A) Stage 4 sleep
(B) Stage 3 sleep
(C) Stage 2 sleep
(D) Stage 1 sleep
(E) REM sleep

87. When in this stage of sleep, brain waves have a fast frequency and low amplitude and look very similar to beta waves, which occur when you are wide-awake and alert. Which state of sleep is this?

(A) Stage 1 sleep
(B) Stage 2 sleep
(C) Stage 3 sleep
(D) REM sleep
(E) Stage 4 sleep

88. Sleepwalking and sleep talking are characteristics of which stage of sleep?

(A) Stage 1 sleep
(B) Stage 2 sleep
(C) Stage 3 sleep
(D) Stage 4 sleep
(E) REM sleep

89. An infant sleeps approximately 17 hours a day. Of those hours, how many are spent in REM?

(A) 20 percent
(B) 30 percent
(C) 50 percent
(D) 70 percent
(E) 80 percent

90. The adaptive sleep theory suggests:

(A) Daily activities deplete key factors in our brain and body that are replenished by sleep.
(B) Sleep evolved because it prevented early humans and animals from wasting energy and exposing themselves to dangers of nocturnal predators.
(C) For our internal clocks to have synchrony with the external world, thereby decreasing fatigue, disorientation, and lack of concentration, sleep is necessary.
(D) Sleep is necessary to combat insomnia and drowsiness.
(E) External environments are constantly competing with individual sleep rhythms. Sleep is necessary to compete with the external clock.

91. The center of the activation-synthesis hypothesis of dreaming is based on the belief that:

(A) The conscious needs to express unfulfilled wishes.
(B) Dreams provide an outlet for repressed thoughts.
(C) Dreams provide explanations for physiological activity.
(D) The unconscious needs to exhibit socially unacceptable behavior.
(E) Dreams allow the individual to work out daily hassles.

92. The majority of our dreams occur in which stage of sleep?

(A) REM sleep
(B) Stage 1 sleep
(C) Stage 2 sleep
(D) Stage 3 sleep
(E) Stage 4 sleep

93. The idea that dreams represent wish fulfillment comes from which theory of dream interpretation?

(A) Extension of waking life
(B) Activation synthesis
(C) Spiritual world
(D) Transformation dream analysis
(E) Freud's theory of dream interpretation

94. Repeated periods during sleep when a person stops breathing for 10 seconds or longer is known as:

(A) Narcolepsy
(B) Sleep apnea
(C) Sleep agnosia
(D) Insomnia
(E) Night terrors

95. A person experiences blind panic, screaming, and thrashing around while sleeping. This episode is called:

(A) A night terror
(B) A nightmare
(C) A sleep terror
(D) Dreaming
(E) A REM rebound episode

96. A relatively rare condition that involves irresistible attacks of sleepiness, brief periods of REM, and often muscle paralysis is called:

(A) Sleep apnea
(B) Sleep terror
(C) Narcolepsy
(D) Benzodiazepines
(E) Night terror

97. REM sleep is also known as paradoxical sleep because:

(A) Measures of the brain activity closely resemble waking consciousness, but the person is in the deepest stage of sleep.
(B) Measures of the brain activity closely resemble waking consciousness, but the person is incapable of moving.
(C) The person's heart rate is slower than when awake, but the person can sleepwalk or sleep talk.
(D) The person can have night terrors during this stage but will not remember them in the morning.
(E) The person's vital signs are very slow, but the person can get up and walk around.

98. The mental state that encompasses the thoughts, feelings, and perceptions that occur when we are reasonably alert is called:

(A) Altered state of consciousness
(B) Subconscious
(C) Preconscious
(D) Alert consciousness
(E) Waking consciousness

99. Alteration in consciousness that occurs seemingly without effort, typically when we want to momentarily escape reality, is called:

(A) Daydreaming
(B) Dreaming
(C) Meditation
(D) Hypnosis
(E) Anesthesia

100. A sleep disorder characterized by difficulty in falling asleep or remaining asleep is called:

(A) Narcoplepsy
(B) Sleep apnea
(C) Insomnia
(D) Sleep terror
(E) Nightmares

101. Which of the following is not a characteristic of REM sleep?

(A) Rapid eye movement
(B) Vivid dreams
(C) Increased heart rate
(D) Paralysis
(E) Delta waves

102. Approximately how many cycles of sleep does an adult enter during a full night's sleep?

(A) One to two
(B) Three to four
(C) Four to five
(D) Six to seven
(E) Seven to eight

103. Approximately how long is each cycle of sleep during a full night's sleep?

(A) 80 minutes
(B) 90 minutes
(C) 60 minutes
(D) 70 minutes
(E) 50 minutes

104. Experimenters have shown that a person deprived of the ______________ stage of sleep will become anxious, testy, and hungry and have difficulty concentrating.

(A) REM
(B) Stage 1
(C) Stage 2
(D) Stage 3
(E) Stage 4

105. Before entering sleep, you briefly pass through a relaxed and drowsy state. This is marked by which characteristic?

(A) Beta waves
(B) Delta waves
(C) Alpha waves
(D) Theta waves
(E) Zeta waves

106. Which part of the brain is important in keeping the forebrain alert and producing a state of wakefulness?

(A) Hippocampus
(B) Limbic system
(C) Hindbrain
(D) Reticular formation
(E) Medulla

107. The dream theory that suggests our dreams reflect the same thoughts, fears, and concerns present when we are awake is called:

(A) Freud's theory of dreams
(B) Extension of waking life
(C) Activation-synthesis
(D) External world
(E) Spiritual world

108. Eighty percent of our sleep takes place in which cycle of sleep?

(A) Stage 1
(B) Stage 2
(C) Stage 3
(D) Stage 4
(E) All of the above

109. Beta waves are characteristic of a person who is:

(A) Dreaming
(B) In a coma
(C) Asleep but not dreaming
(D) Awake and alert
(E) In stage 1 sleep

110. ________________ refers to an increased percentage of time spent in REM sleep when we are deprived of REM sleep on the previous night.

(A) REM rebound
(B) REM deprivation
(C) REM sleep
(D) REM makeup
(E) REM extension

CHAPTER 7

Drugs and Hypnosis

111. According to Ernest Hilgard's hidden observer theory, people who are hypnotized and told to plunge one hand into a glass of painfully cold ice water with the suggestion they will not feel pain, will respond to the question "Do you feel pain?" by:

(A) Saying they do not feel pain
(B) Waking up from the hypnotic trance
(C) Screaming and removing their hand from the water
(D) Screaming but leaving their hand in the water
(E) Saying they do feel pain

112. Which of the following drugs are physically addictive?

(A) Morphine
(B) Cocaine
(C) Heroin
(D) All of these
(E) None of these

113. Which statement best defines dependency?

(A) The original dosage of the drug no longer produces desired effects.
(B) Behavioral patterns are marked by overwhelming desire to obtain and use the drug.
(C) A change in the nervous system occurs so that a person now needs to take the drug to prevent withdrawal symptoms.
(D) Painful physical and psychological symptoms occur after the drug is no longer in the system.
(E) Decompression from the peripheral nervous system begins after the drug enters the body.

114. Which of the following drugs block reuptake, leading to increased neural stimulation?

(A) Heroin
(B) Cocaine
(C) Morphine
(D) Amphetamines
(E) Methamphetamines

115. Which of the following drugs does not fall under the category of a stimulant?

(A) Cocaine
(B) Caffeine
(C) Nicotine
(D) Amphetamines
(E) Heroin

116. The reduction in the body's response to a drug, which may accompany continual drug use, is called:

(A) Withdrawal
(B) Addiction
(C) Dependency
(D) Tolerance
(E) Hallucinations

117. A teenage boy once described using this drug as "life without anxiety, . . . it makes you feel good." However, this boy eventually discovered the dark side of the drug. With constant use, dosages became larger and larger. Eventually getting high was almost impossible and normal functioning was out of the question. Which drug was he referring to?

(A) Cocaine
(B) Nicotine
(C) Heroin
(D) LSD
(E) Psilocybin

118. Hallucinogens are best defined as:

(A) Psychoactive drugs that produce strange and unusual perceptual, sensory, and cognitive experiences
(B) Stimulants that produce arousals both physically and psychologically
(C) Designer drugs that cause three primary effects, pain reduction, euphoria, and tolerance
(D) Mild depressants that decrease heart rate and blood pressure
(E) Drugs that stimulate the central nervous system

119. In order for a person to be hypnotized, the hypnotist must do which of the following?

(A) Suggest what the subject will experience during hypnosis
(B) Tell the subject what he or she will be doing while under hypnosis
(C) Tell the subject to count from ten to one
(D) Suggest that the subject enter a trance
(E) Tell the subject to relax and feel no stress

120. Which age group of people is most susceptible to hypnosis?

(A) 20–24
(B) 17–20
(C) 15–19
(D) 8–12
(E) 45–49

121. Cold sweats, vomiting, convulsions, and hallucinations are all symptoms of what drug?

(A) LSD
(B) Cocaine
(C) Methamphetamines
(D) Barbiturates
(E) Heroin

122. ________________ are psychoactive drugs that depress the central nervous system, while ________________ stimulate the central nervous system.

(A) Opiates, barbiturates
(B) Opiates, amphetamines
(C) Barbiturates, amphetamines
(D) Amphetamines, barbiturates
(E) Amphetamines, opiates

123. What are the four major areas of impact of psychoactive drugs?

(A) Appetite, behavior, sex drive, and perception
(B) Perception, behavior, moods, mental processes
(C) Perception, mental processes, appetite, digestion
(D) Appetite, perception, moods, mental processes
(E) Mental processes, moods, digestion, perception

124. Which of the following psychoactive drugs is *not* a depressant?

(A) Alcohol
(B) Barbiturates
(C) Benzodiazepines
(D) Heroin
(E) Nembutal

125. This drug induces a number of physiological and psychological effects, some of which include dilated blood vessels in the eye, dry mouth, time distortion, euphoric feelings, sense of relaxation, and mild muscular weakness.

(A) Alcohol
(B) Marijuana
(C) LSD
(D) Tranquilizers
(E) Cocaine

126. Which of the following is *not* a practical application of hypnosis?

(A) Ease pain
(B) Stop smoking
(C) Remember a painful event
(D) Stop overeating
(E) Marriage counseling

127. In the 1700s a force called "animal magnetism," later known as hypnosis, was introduced by:

(A) Sigmund Freud
(B) Ernest Hilgard
(C) Wilhelm Wundt
(D) William James
(E) Anton Mesmer

128. In using hypnosis for pain reduction, patients highly susceptible to hypnosis were:

(A) More likely to experience posthypnotic amnesia
(B) Less likely to participate in future studies
(C) More likely to report significantly lower pain levels
(D) Less likely to report lower pain levels
(E) Likely to respond more slowly to the induction method

129. All of the following are terms related to hypnosis *except*:

(A) Posthypnotic amnesia
(B) Hidden observer
(C) Suggestibility
(D) Hypnotic analgesia
(E) Posthypnotic exhortation

130. Which of the following statements best describes opiates?

(A) Opiates will not produce withdrawal.
(B) Opiates are not very addictive.
(C) Marijuana is an example of an opiate.
(D) Opiates are only psychologically addictive.
(E) Heroin is an example of an opiate.

CHAPTER 8

Classical Conditioning

131. A group of ranchers attempts to discourage coyotes from attacking their sheep by placing a substance on the wool of the sheep that makes coyotes violently ill if they eat it. Very quickly, the coyotes avoid the sheep entirely. In this scenario, what are the UCS, CS, and CR, respectively?

(A) The substance, the sheep's wool, aversion to the sheep
(B) The sheep's wool, the substance, aversion to sheep
(C) Aversion to sheep, the substance, the sheep's wool
(D) The coyotes, the sheep's wool, aversion to sheep
(E) The substance, the sheep's wool, the coyotes

132. The same ranchers discover that now not only will the coyotes not attack the treated sheep but also they will not attack nearby sheep. This is an example of:

(A) Extinction
(B) Discrimination
(C) Generalization
(D) Spontaneous recovery
(E) Chaining

133. In operant conditioning, the Premack Principle states that:

(A) Punishment is ineffective.
(B) Primary reinforcers are used to reinforce desirable behavior.
(C) Punishment is effective when paired with an adversive stimulus.
(D) Acquiring a desired behavior from an individual can be effectively used as a reinforcer for another, less desirable activity.
(E) More desirable behavior can be achieved through positive reinforcement.

134. Mrs. Jackson, an English teacher, gives pop quizzes to her students every marking period. This is an example of:

(A) Variable interval schedule of reinforcement
(B) Variable ratio schedule of reinforcement
(C) Fixed ratio schedule of reinforcement
(D) Fixed interval schedule of reinforcement
(E) Interval ratio schedule of reinforcement

135. In what manner would Ivan Pavlov have conducted extinction trials on his classically conditioned dogs?

(A) Reinforcing the behavior he wished to extinguish
(B) Repeatedly presenting the conditioned stimulus (bell) without pairing it with the unconditioned stimulus (food)
(C) Repeatedly presenting dogs with the food and the bell at the same time
(D) Immediately giving the dogs food (UCS) after the bell (CS) rings
(E) Repeatedly bringing in different types of food (UCS) and then reinforcing the salivating immediately after

136. In John Watson's "Little Albert" experiment, what was the UCS?

(A) The white rat
(B) The little boy
(C) Anything white and furry
(D) The loud noise
(E) Fear

137. Which of the following is true of classical conditioning?

(A) UCS produces UCR
(B) CR produces the CS
(C) UCR produces the CS
(D) CS produces the UCS
(E) UCR produces the UCS

138. Dylan's mother buys him a sailor's cap before they go on a family fishing trip. On the boat, Dylan gets nauseated and vomits. The next day he gets nauseated just from looking at the sailor's cap. The sailor's cap has become:

(A) The unconditioned stimulus
(B) The conditioned stimulus
(C) The conditioned response
(D) The unconditioned response
(E) The reconditioned stimulus

139. Before Dylan became nauseated, he was able to go fishing with his family, even catching several fish. Fishing is an example of what schedule of reinforcement?

(A) Fixed ratio
(B) Fixed interval
(C) Unfixed interval
(D) Variable ratio
(E) Variable interval

140. Sean sells shoes for a living. His salary depends on how many shoes he can sell in a two-week period of time. What schedule of reinforcement is Sean being paid with?

(A) Variable ratio
(B) Variable interval
(C) Fixed ratio
(D) Fixed interval
(E) None of the above

141. A passenger on an airplane was feeling very anxious about an important job interview the next morning, and as a result he was uneasy and nervous the entire flight. Back home a week later, he is contemplating a holiday trip. Though he hadn't previously been afraid to fly, he finds himself suddenly nervous about flying and decides to cancel his plans to visit an out-of-state relative. What are the UCS, UCR, CS, and CR, respectively?

(A) Job interview, feeling nervous and anxious, flying, feeling nervous and anxious about flying
(B) Feeling nervous and anxious, flying, out-of-state relative, feeling anxious and nervous about flying
(C) Flying, feeling nervous and anxious, job interview, feeling nervous and anxious
(D) Feeling nervous and anxious, job interview, flying, feeling nervous and anxious
(E) Job interview, feeling nervous and anxious, out-of-state relative, feeling nervous and anxious

142. As part of a new and intriguing line of research in behavioral medicine, researchers gave mice saccharine-flavored water and followed it up with an injection of a drug that weakens mice's immune systems. Later, when these mice drank saccharine-flavored water, they showed signs of weakened immune response. Research is currently under way to see if the reverse is possible (if conditioning can be used to increase immune functioning), a discovery that would surely have important implications for new medical treatments. In this experiment, what is the saccharine-flavored water?

(A) Unconditioned stimulus
(B) Conditioned stimulus
(C) Conditioned response
(D) Unconditioned response
(E) Stimulus response

143. Automobile advertisements, especially those for sports cars, often feature young, beautiful women. Smart advertisers know and research confirms that men rate new cars whose ads include an attractive female as faster, more appealing, better designed, and more desirable than cars with similar ads that do not include an attractive female. What is the unconditioned response?

(A) The car
(B) The advertisement
(C) The attractive women
(D) Desire to buy the car
(E) Finding the woman attractive

144. In the preceding scenario, in terms of classical conditioning, what is the attractive woman?

(A) The conditioned stimulus
(B) The unconditioned stimulus
(C) The conditioned response
(D) The unconditioned response
(E) The stimulus response

145. Which of the following statements best defines

(A) A type of learning in which behaviors ar and punishments

(B) A type of learning based on modeling or imita others

(C) A type of learning in which a response naturally elicite comes to be elicited by a formerly neutral stimulus

(D) The process by which experience or practice results in a change behavior

(E) The process by which voluntary behaviors are produced in the presence of certain stimuli

146. During the conditioning process of Pavlov's dogs, what element of classical conditioning did the bell and food play?

(A) CS and UCS

(B) US and CS

(C) UCS and CS

(D) CS and UCR

(E) CS and CR

147. Desensitization therapy can best be defined as:

(A) A conditioning technique that creates an avoidance of certain foods

(B) A conditioning technique that creates a conditioned response from a formerly neutral stimuli

(C) A conditioning technique that gradually increases one's desire to perform a particular behavior

(D) A conditioning technique that uses generalization to get people to overcome their fears

(E) A conditioning technique designed to gradually reduce anxiety about a particular object or situation

148. Classical conditioning would best be suited to answer which of the following questions?

(A) Why do people repeat behaviors when they are followed by something good?

(B) Why do children know a lot about driving a car before their first time behind the wheel?

(C) Why do people associate certain foods with nausea?

(D) Why are some animals difficult to train to perform certain kinds of behaviors?

(E) Why do people imitate behaviors they see someone else get punished for?

Of the following, which would a psychologist consider the best example of learning?

(A) A young man's beard beginning to grow at age 15
(B) A woman experiencing labor pains
(C) Salmon swimming upstream during the mating season
(D) A child being able to ride a bike
(E) A baby sucking on her mother's breast for nourishment

150. The sight of a needle can trigger fear in some people. Why is this an example of classical conditioning?

(A) People learn this when they are young.
(B) There is an unconditioned association with fear and the needle.
(C) Needles hurt.
(D) With positive reinforcement one can overcome their fear.
(E) As people get older they overcome this fear.

CHAPTER 9

Operant Conditioning and Cognitive Learning

151. What is one major difference between operant conditioning and classical conditioning?

(A) Operant conditioning takes place as a result of some voluntary action, while classical conditioning takes place without choice.
(B) Operant conditioning takes place before the response, while classical conditioning takes place after the response.
(C) Operant conditioning is learned by association, while classical conditioning is learned by reinforcement.
(D) Classical conditioning is part of social cognitive learning, while operant conditioning is not.
(E) Classical conditioning has a stimulus but no response, while operant conditioning has both a stimulus and a response.

152. Suspending a basketball player for committing a flagrant foul is an example of:

(A) Negative reinforcement
(B) Positive reinforcement
(C) Punishment
(D) Primary reinforcement
(E) Secondary reinforcement

153. A defendant is harassed and tortured until he confesses. This is an example of:

(A) Positive reinforcement
(B) Negative reinforcement
(C) Punishment
(D) Positive punishment
(E) Negative punishment

154. Punishment can best be defined as:

(A) The reinforcement of a behavior every time it occurs
(B) Taking away something unpleasant when the subject performs the correct behavior
(C) An attempt to weaken a response by following it with something unpleasant
(D) Adding something unwanted when the subject is not doing the correct behavior and then stopping it when he or she displays the correct behavior
(E) Anything that comes to represent a primary reinforcer

155. Which of the following statements best explains E. L. Thorndike's law of effect?

(A) Behaviors that are negatively reinforced are more likely to discontinue than behaviors that are punished.
(B) Receiving reinforcement every time a person performs a good deed, continuous reinforcement, will increase the likelihood that the person will continue that behavior.
(C) The stimuli of food, water, and sex are innately satisfying and require no learning.
(D) Behaviors are strengthened by positive consequences and weakened by negative ones.
(E) Behaviors are reinforced through primary reinforcers.

156. B. F. Skinner used his "Skinner Box" to work on a procedure in which the experimenter successfully reinforced behaviors, which led up to the desired behavior. This procedure is known as:

(A) Reinforcement
(B) Chaining
(C) Primary reinforcers
(D) Secondary reinforcers
(E) Shaping

157. Schedules of reinforcement have a direct effect on maintaining your behavior. Which of the following schedules of reinforcement is identified in this example: Calling a friend and getting a busy signal because he or she is frequently on the phone?

(A) Fixed interval
(B) Variable interval
(C) Fixed ratio
(D) Variable ratio
(E) Fixed variable

158. Which of the following is the best example of a negative reinforcement?

(A) A child getting spanked for bad behavior
(B) A kindergarten student being put in "time-out"
(C) A teenager not being allowed to go to her friend's party
(D) A mother taking an aspirin to eliminate her headache
(E) A father getting a speeding ticket

159. Which of the following best describes the basic principle behind operant conditioning?

(A) The consequences one receives are directly based on his or her behavior.
(B) The conditioned stimulus one responds to is called a conditioned response.
(C) Continuous reinforcement is the best way to reinforce positive behavior.
(D) To decrease undesired behaviors one must use negative punishment.
(E) Negative reinforcement and punishment both equally help to rid unwanted behavior.

160. What is the goal of both positive and negative reinforcement?

(A) To decrease the likelihood that a negative reinforcer will follow a behavior
(B) To increase the likelihood that the preceding behavior will be repeated
(C) To decrease the likelihood that the preceding behavior will be repeated
(D) To ensure there are no negative consequences following the behavior
(E) To add a primary reinforcer after someone does a proper behavior

161. Latent learning can best be described as:

(A) Learning that depends on the mental process
(B) Learning that is not immediately reflected in a behavior change
(C) A learning technique that provides precise information about one's inner bodily functions
(D) Learning that is based on rewards and punishments
(E) A type of learning that occurs after the behavior has already been done

162. Thorndike's law of effect neglects the inner drives or motives that make learners pursue the "satisfying state," allowing learners to reach their goals. Which of the following psychologists would have agreed with that statement?

(A) Kohler
(B) Pavlov
(C) Tolman
(D) Skinner
(E) Watson

163. Which of the following scenarios is the best example of a cognitive map?

(A) A dog sits by the window an hour before her owner should return home.
(B) A little girl remembers to get her jacket before leaving for school.
(C) A boy follows his big sister home on his bicycle.
(D) When asked for directions to his job, a man recites them in great detail.
(E) A teacher remembers all the names of her students.

164. Wolfgang Kohler conducted a series of experiments in which he placed a chimpanzee in a cage with a banana on the ground just out of his reach outside of the cage. After a period of inaction, the chimp suddenly grabbed the stick in the cage, poked it through the cage, and dragged the banana within reach. This type of learning is called:

(A) Insight
(B) Latent
(C) Cognitive
(D) Operant
(E) Observational

165. Harry Harlows's goal was to get his monkeys to figure out that in any set of six trials, the food was always under the same box. Initially the monkeys chose the boxes randomly, sometimes finding food and sometimes not. However, after a while their behavior changed: after two consistent trials of finding the correct box, they continually went back to the same box. Harlow concluded that the monkeys had "learned how to learn." According to Harlow the monkeys established:

(A) Cognitive maps
(B) Reinforcers
(C) Cognitive sets
(D) Learned maps
(E) Learning sets

166. Which of the following statements best exemplifies the idea behind social cognitive learning?

(A) Learning occurs when we see someone else being punished for a behavior.
(B) Learning is likely to happen whether we see someone else punished or rewarded for behavior.
(C) Learning occurs when we see someone else being rewarded for a behavior.
(D) Learning is simply based on observation.
(E) Learning is based on external rewards and behaviors.

167. In Albert Bandura's "bobo" doll experiment, which group of children spontaneously acted aggressively toward the doll rather quickly?

(A) Model-reward condition
(B) Model-punished condition
(C) No-consequences condition
(D) Reward and punishment condition
(E) No condition

168. Devyn watches a violent television show and then pretends to shoot her brother Tyler with a toy pistol. A psychologist would say that Devyn has learned this behavior through:

(A) Operant conditioning
(B) Classical conditioning
(C) Vicarious learning
(D) Latent learning
(E) Learning set

169. Which of the following psychologists would argue that learning can take place when someone is watching another person and performs that behavior even when not reinforced?

(A) Edward Tolman
(B) Wolfgang Kohler
(C) B. F. Skinner
(D) John Watson
(E) Albert Bandura

170. Which of the following responses is *not* learned through operant conditioning?

(A) Shelly gets $50 after getting a 90 percent in her math class.
(B) A pigeon learns to peck a disc to get food pellets.
(C) A dog learns to turn in circles for a reward.
(D) A baby takes his first steps.
(E) A horse jumps over a fence to avoid an electric shock.

171. Joey is refusing to complete his homework on time. After learning about Joey's love of trains, Mrs. Anderson promises to reward Joey with a Thomas and Friends video upon completion of his next two homework assignments. This is an example of:

(A) Positive reinforcement
(B) Generalization
(C) Insight
(D) Latent learning
(E) The Premack Principle

172. While taking his math placement exam, Spencer became stuck on one problem. With only five minutes left, he suddenly arrived at the answer. This is an example of:

(A) Latent learning
(B) Insight
(C) Learning set
(D) Abstract learning
(E) Operant conditioning

173. After several attempts at escape with no success, the electrically shocked dogs give up. At that moment the gates open and the dogs could simply walk out, but they don't; instead they just sit there. This could most likely be explained by the concept of:

(A) Latent learning
(B) Spontaneous recovery
(C) Vicarious learning
(D) Learned helplessness
(E) Intrinsic motivation

174. After overcoming her fear of the dentist, Jada finds out she needs a root canal. On her way to the dentist's office, her old fears and anxieties return and she begins to panic. This is an example of:

(A) Generalization
(B) Spontaneous recovery
(C) Discrimination
(D) Insight
(E) Classical conditioning

175. Salina receives a one-thousand-dollar bonus at her job after she sold the most cars this month. The one-thousand-dollar bonus is an example of a:

(A) Primary reinforcer
(B) Secondary reinforcer
(C) Partial reinforcer
(D) Continual reinforcer
(E) Total reinforcer

CHAPTER 10

Memory

176. Katie was able to remember the number 111 by associating it with Admiral Nelson, who happened to have one eye, one arm, and one leg. This is an example of:

(A) Retrieving
(B) Storing
(C) Encoding
(D) Memory
(E) Imagery

177. Which of the following examples best illustrates episodic memory?

(A) Remembering that you got a bicycle for your 12th birthday
(B) Knowing that Christopher Columbus sailed in 1492
(C) Teaching someone how to play tennis
(D) Reciting the alphabet
(E) Understanding a conversation someone is having in a foreign language

178. When asked why she fears spiders, Sophia is unable to explain her fears, where they came from, or how she got them. This is an example of:

(A) Semantic memory, which helps us avoid painful memories
(B) Episodic memory, which has knowledge of specific personal memories
(C) Procedural memory, which holds memories that we are not aware of
(D) Echoic memory, which holds memories we cannot retrieve
(E) Iconic memory, which allows us to forget fear-inducing thoughts

179. Which of the following brain structures plays an important role in memory storage, from STM to LTM?

(A) Thalamus
(B) Hypothalamus
(C) Amygdala
(D) Hippocampus
(E) Cerebrum

180. Suppose you are absorbed in reading a novel and a friend asks you a question. You stop reading and ask, "What did you say?" As soon as the words leave your mouth, you realize you can recall your friend's exact words. What is the reason for your ability to play back these words?

(A) Iconic memory
(B) Echoic memory
(C) Semantic memory
(D) Sensory memory
(E) Short-term memory

181. According to the information-processing model, which is the correct order of inputting information?

(A) Encode semantically, retrieve elaborately, store information
(B) Retrieve from long-term memory, encode in short-term memory, encode in sensory memory
(C) Encode in sensory memory, encode in short-term memory, encode in long-term memory
(D) Store information, retrieve upon demand, encode necessary information
(E) Encode with sensory receptors, store information, retrieve upon demand

182. Which of the following statements is *not* true?

(A) Deep processing involves elaborate rehearsal.
(B) Automatic processing is unconscious encoding of information.
(C) Interference results when new information enters short-term memory and pushes out old information.
(D) Levels of processing theory says that remembering depends on how information is encoded.
(E) Declarative memory involves memories for skills, habits, and things learned through classical conditioning.

183. While walking home from a party drunk, Jeff witnessed a crime. When questioned by the police the following day, he could not remember what he saw. After drinking some liquor, Jeff remembered the crime. This phenomenon best illustrates:

(A) The framing effect
(B) Short-term memory loss
(C) Hypnotic amnesia
(D) State-dependent memory
(E) Anterograde amnesia

184. Which type of memory is also referred to as working memory?

(A) Long-term memory
(B) Short-term memory
(C) Sensory memory
(D) Semantic memory
(E) Episodic memory

185. The ability to maintain exact detailed visual memories over a significant period of time is called:

(A) Flashbulb memory
(B) Semantic memory
(C) Eidetic memory
(D) Echoic memory
(E) Iconic memory

186. The amygdala is responsible for which of the following types of memories?

(A) Emotional
(B) Procedural
(C) Factual
(D) Iconic
(E) Visual

187. The primacy effect is best explained by which of the following statements?

(A) Items on a list with unique meaning are more likely to be remembered.
(B) The first items on a list are likely to be more effectively rehearsed and therefore more likely to be remembered.
(C) Items on a list presented more recently are more likely to be remembered.
(D) Items on a list with simplistic meaning are more likely to be remembered.
(E) The last items on a list are more likely to be encoded first and therefore remembered.

188. During his English class, Ben is able to recall the author of *The Scarlet Letter*. This type of memory is called:

(A) Procedural
(B) Episodic
(C) Long term
(D) Semantic
(E) Constructive

189. Which of the following statements best explains one major difference between short-term memory and long-term memory?

(A) Long-term memory is unlimited in capacity while short-term memory is not.
(B) Long-term memory holds only episodic memories while short-term memory does not.
(C) Long-term memory varies a great deal from one person to another, while short-term memory does not.
(D) In terms of processing, long-term memory comes directly after sensory memory while short-term memory does not.
(E) Long-term memory depends on neural connections in the limbic system while short-term memory does not.

190. Maintenance rehearsal involves:

(A) Recalling the words at the end of a list
(B) Intentionally repeating information
(C) Processing visual memories
(D) Systematically recalling information
(E) Processing iconic memories

191. Linda looks up a telephone number for take-out pizza. She repeats it over and over as she dials the number. However, after giving her order and hanging up, she has forgotten the number. This is an example of the use of what memory process?

(A) Short-term memory
(B) Sensory memory
(C) Automatic processing
(D) Echoic memory
(E) Iconic memory

192. After forgetting the combination to several other locks, Nate was trying to find a way to remember the combination to the new lock he bought last week. The combination is 19, 20, 9. To remember the combination, he thinks of the year 1929. His method to remember this is an example of:

(A) Elaborate rehearsal
(B) Maintenance rehearsal
(C) Short-term memory
(D) Chunking
(E) Decoding

193. The process of encoding information from short-term memory to long-term memory is most efficient when it:

(A) Has a procedural manner
(B) Involves some kind of association
(C) Uses repetition
(D) Does not use repetition
(E) Uses semantic memory

194. Maintenance rehearsal is to elaborate rehearsal as:

(A) Long-term memory is to short-term memory
(B) Sensory memory is to long-term memory
(C) Short-term memory is to long-term memory
(D) Sensory memory is to short-term memory
(E) Automatic memory is to long-term memory

195. Which of the following is *not* an example of effortful encoding?

(A) Maintenance rehearsal
(B) Repetition
(C) Meaningful associations
(D) Chunking
(E) Transferring information from STM to LTM

CHAPTER 11

Remembering and Forgetting

196. Which of the following statements is correct regarding why eyewitness testimony is not always accurate?

(A) People do not have the capacity to remember.
(B) People may be asked misleading questions.
(C) People do not have a strong recognition.
(D) People do not have a strong ability to recall past information.
(E) People lie too often.

197. What is the correct name of the memory files that contain related information about a specific topic or category?

(A) Prototypes
(B) Nerve cells
(C) Nodes
(D) Networks
(E) Schemas

198. One of the earliest psychologists to study memory and forgetting was Herman Ebbinghaus, who used himself as a subject to test his own recall of a list of nonsense syllables, previously learned through rehearsal. From his work he came up with the concept of a forgetting curve. This suggests:

(A) Remembering nonsense syllables can be encoded faster than meaningful information.
(B) Old information will interfere with new information being encoded into LTM.
(C) New information will interfere with old information already stored in LTM.
(D) Recall of meaningless information drops very soon after initial learning and then levels off.
(E) Recall of meaningless information cannot be retrieved more than three hours after encoding.

199. Maya is currently enrolled in an Italian class at her local college. While on spring break, Maya travels to Italy. She is excited to practice her new skills, but when she gets there she is having trouble. Every time she tries to speak Italian, Spanish words she learned in high school come out. This is an example of:

(A) Retroactive interference
(B) Proactive interference
(C) Retrograde amnesia
(D) Anterograde amnesia
(E) Dissociative interference

200. Retrograde amnesia can best be defined as:

(A) Memory loss for events that occur after the time of the incident
(B) Memory loss that occurs from childbirth
(C) Memory loss for events that have occurred before the time of the incident
(D) Memory loss without any specific cause
(E) Memory loss for events that have occurred before and after the incident

201. Jayden consciously pushes the due date for his term project out of his mind, so much so that on the day it is due, Jayden must take an incomplete from his teacher. This is an example of:

(A) Repression
(B) Aggression
(C) Amnesia
(D) Forgetting
(E) Suppression

202. After his car accident, Paul cannot make any new memories. In fact, to remember his daily activities Paul must write everything down. This is known as:

(A) Retrograde amnesia
(B) Anterograde amnesia
(C) Proactive interference
(D) Retroactive interference
(E) Dissociative amnesia

203. The method of loci includes which of the following three steps?

(A) Create visual places, memorize those places, create vivid imagery
(B) Create vivid associations, memorize visual sequences, put associations into places
(C) Memorize visual sequence of places, create vivid associations, put associations into selected places
(D) Memorize selected places, create vivid imagery, memorize vivid imagery
(E) Create vivid associations, memorize associations, put associations into places

204. The ability to transfer information about words, facts, and events (declarative information) from STM to LTM depends on activity in which part of the brain?

(A) Hypothalamus
(B) Thalamus
(C) Amygdala
(D) Hippocampus
(E) Medulla

205. Talking to yourself over and over again, repeating information silently or out loud, is called:

(A) Elaborate rehearsal
(B) Rote rehearsal
(C) Procedural memory
(D) Declarative memory
(E) Semantic memory

206. Subjects in an experiment learned a sequence of letters (PSQ). Then they were given a three-digit number (167) and asked to count backwards by threes: 167, 164, 161, and so on, for 18 seconds. At the end they were asked to recall the three letters. The subjects showed a rapid decline in their ability to remember the letters. This phenomenon is known as:

(A) Proactive interference
(B) Retroactive interference
(C) Decay theory
(D) Forgetting curve
(E) Episodic interference

207. Which of the following exemplifies retrograde interference?

(A) Ella failed her French test because she was confusing it with Spanish words she studied last year.
(B) Ava, a medical student, failed her test on the bones in the hand because she studied for the bones in the foot after studying the hand.
(C) Isabella can no longer form new memories after her head trauma.
(D) Nya remembers only the last three items her mom put on the grocery shopping list.
(E) Emma cannot remember her third-grade teacher's name, but she does remember her fourth-grade teacher's name.

208. After studying for a test, Jack realized he remembered exactly where a particular piece of information appeared on a page in his textbook, even though he did not try to remember the item. This is an example of:

(A) Explicit memory
(B) Procedural memory
(C) Declarative memory
(D) Implicit memory
(E) Semantic memory

209. Recognition involves which of the following?

(A) Retrieving previously learned information without the presence of any cues
(B) Using the available cues to identify information that has already been learned
(C) Filling in a specific amount of information without the use of any newly learned cues
(D) Using available cues to create an entirely new response
(E) Encoding new information to replace previously learned information

210. Corey sits at his kitchen table to think about what he needs to buy at the grocery store. He is using his ability to:

(A) Recognize
(B) Recite
(C) Memorize
(D) Recall
(E) Initiate

211. After making a mess of the playroom, Mason visualizes where each toy should be placed in the room. He is using:

(A) Method of loci
(B) Peg method
(C) Visualization
(D) Elaborate rehearsal
(E) Procedural memory

212. Based on Herman Ebbinghaus's forgetting curve research using nonsense syllables, unfamiliar information is:

(A) Forgotten within the first eight hours
(B) Forgotten within the first hour
(C) Forgotten within the first day
(D) Forgotten within the first two days
(E) Forgotten within the first week

213. The forgetting curve measures which of the following?

(A) The amount of previously learned information that subjects remember across time
(B) The amount of new information that can remain in the short-term memory
(C) Memory that cannot be consciously remembered over time
(D) The amount of information children can retain over age five
(E) The amount of information one can memorize in any given day

214. Recognition is to recall as:

(A) Fill-in is to multiple choice
(B) Fill-in is to essay
(C) Multiple choice is to fill-in
(D) Multiple choice is to essay
(E) Multiple choice is to matching

215. Kimberly knows she did something embarrassing at her friend's birthday party many years before, but she cannot remember what it was. This is an example of:

(A) Repression
(B) Amnesia
(C) Forgetting curve
(D) Implicit memory
(E) Interference

CHAPTER 12

Intelligence and Testing

216. Mental age can best be defined as:

(A) A method of estimating a child's intellectual ability by comparing the child's score on intelligence tests and his or her age
(B) A method of estimating a child's intellectual ability based on raw scores on intelligence tests
(C) Comparing a child's actual age with his or her computed age
(D) Basing a child's age level on his or her scores on a standardized test
(E) Charting a child's age based on the level of correct responses on an intelligence test

217. When an intelligence test measures what it is supposed to, the test is considered to be:

(A) Reliable
(B) Valid
(C) Accurate
(D) Standardized
(E) Comparative

218. Which of the following psychologists believed that intelligence was a collection of mental abilities?

(A) Wechsler
(B) Broca
(C) Binet
(D) Terman
(E) Galton

219. The extent to which traits, abilities, or IQ scores may increase or decrease as a result of environmental factors is called:

(A) Nature-nurture question
(B) Heritability
(C) Independent variables
(D) Reaction range
(E) Ecological testing

220. If a four-year-old girl correctly answered questions on an intelligence exam similar to a five-year-old girl, she would be said to have a mental age of five. In this case her intelligence quotient (IQ) would be:

(A) 100
(B) 95
(C) 150
(D) 125
(E) 110

221. Which of the following psychologists added a performance scale in an attempt to measure nonverbal skills and rule out other cultural or educational biases?

(A) Wechsler
(B) Binet
(C) Gardner
(D) Sternberg
(E) Terman

222. Charles Spearman's two-factor theory of intelligence referred to which of the following?

(A) Mathematical skills and spatial intelligence
(B) Analytical problem solving and interpersonal skills
(C) Ability to perform complex mental work and mathematical or verbal skills
(D) Analytical problem solving and intrapersonal skills
(E) Ability to reason logically and demonstrate written language and thinking skills

223. Robert Sternberg's triarchic theory of intelligence was divided into three categories. Which three categories are correct?

(A) Practical, intrapersonal, creative
(B) Experimental, analytical, problem solving
(C) Experimental, problem solving, practical
(D) Analytical, logical, practical
(E) Analytical, problem solving, practical

224. According to Raymond Cattell, what is the major difference between crystallized intelligence and fluid intelligence?

(A) Crystallized intelligence refers to problem-solving abilities, while fluid intelligence is the ability to absorb and retain information.
(B) Crystallized intelligence is the ability to absorb and retain information, while fluid intelligence refers to problem-solving abilities.
(C) Crystallized intelligence is the ability to be analytical, while fluid intelligence is the ability to read and write.
(D) Crystallized intelligence is the ability to read and write, while fluid intelligence is the ability to be analytical.
(E) Crystallized intelligence is the ability to absorb information, while fluid intelligence is the ability to analyze the information.

225. An architect would likely have good spatial intelligence, a gymnast or dancer would likely have good body-kinesthetic intelligence, and a psychologist would probably have good intrapersonal skills. Which of the following psychologists would agree with this statement?

(A) Gardner
(B) Spearman
(C) Thurstone
(D) Guilford
(E) Terman

226. On a normal distribution of IQ test scores, with a mean of 100 and a standard deviation of 15 points, a score of 85 places you approximately in what percentile of the population?

(A) 16th
(B) 50th
(C) 97th
(D) 76th
(E) 24th

227. Which of the following types of tests measures the capacity of a test taker to perform some task or role in the future?

(A) Achievement
(B) Aptitude
(C) Conventional
(D) Self-monitored
(E) Adult intelligence scale

228. A savant can best be defined as:

(A) A mentally handicapped individual
(B) A child between the ages of 8 and 12 who suffers from autism
(C) A mentally handicapped individual with exceptional ability in mathematical calculations, memory, art, or music
(D) A male adult who suffers from delusional thoughts and erratic behavior
(E) A social loner who has exceptional abilities in the field of science or math

229. Which of the following psychologists did *not* suggest the existence of more than one kind of intelligence?

(A) Gardner
(B) Sternberg
(C) Guilford
(D) Thurstone
(E) Spearman

230. The American Psychiatric Association established IQ ranges for various levels of retardation. Below 25 is considered to be:

(A) Profound retardation
(B) Severe retardation
(C) Mild retardation
(D) Moderate retardation
(E) Extreme retardation

231. The WAIS and the WISC are credited for:

(A) Creating early intervention programs for the mentally ill
(B) Creating intelligence tests specific to different age groups
(C) Creating one standardized test equal for all cultures and races
(D) Creating a new understanding of the term *mental age*
(E) Creating intelligence tests that only test verbal skills

232. The MMPI (Minnesota multiphasic inventories) is designed to:

(A) Measure a person's verbal and mathematical skills
(B) Measure a student's academic potential
(C) Require students to tell stories about a particular photograph
(D) Identify characteristics of personality and behavior
(E) Measure the aptitude of high school students

233. Which of these tests is projective, requiring subjects to tell stories about photographs or drawings?

(A) MMPI
(B) WAIS
(C) TAT
(D) Rorschach Test
(E) Myers-Briggs Type Indicator

234. Which of the following statements best defines the concept of equivalent form reliability?

(A) The score received on the first half of a test should correlate with the score received on the second half of the test.
(B) The score received on a test should correlate with a score received on another test of the same material.
(C) The score a grader assigns to one assessment should match that of another grader.
(D) The score received on the test should reflect the scores received on previous standardized tests.
(E) The score received on the test should reflect current academic achievement.

235. Alfred Binet is known as the father of intelligence mainly because of his work in:

(A) The assessment of one's ability to learn and the creation of the mental age
(B) The creation of the intelligence quotient (IQ)
(C) The creation of both the mental age and the intelligence quotient
(D) The assessment of one's ability to learn and the intelligence quotient
(E) The understanding of the heritability factors in terms of intelligence

236. Because Lela did not want to raise her child in poverty, she put her baby up for adoption. A middle-class family, in a good home, is now raising Lela's baby. What effect could this have on the child's IQ?

(A) It will probably be lower than the IQs of children who stay with their biological parents.
(B) It will not be significantly different from the IQs of children who stay in a disadvantaged setting.
(C) It will be higher than the IQs of children who stay in disadvantaged settings only if adoptive parents have above-average IQs.
(D) It may be as much as 10 to 15 points higher than the IQs of children who stay in disadvantaged settings.
(E) It will make no difference because an individual's IQ is based solely on genetic factors.

237. The concept of reaction range indicates that:

(A) Intelligence is fixed at birth, because it is based on genetic factors.
(B) Intelligence may increase or decrease as a result of the environment.
(C) Intelligence is completely variable due to environmental factors.
(D) Heredity establishes a very narrow range for intellectual development.
(E) Intelligence is completely determined by age five.

238. If genetic factors contribute to IQ scores, then fraternal twins should have:

(A) Less similar IQ scores than identical twins
(B) More similar IQ scores than identical twins
(C) More similar than IQ scores of siblings
(D) Completely different IQ scores
(E) No connection at all

239. In a normal distribution of IQ scores, what percentage of people has a score between 85 and 115?

(A) 35 percent
(B) 54 percent
(C) 68.26 percent
(D) 79.32 percent
(E) 95.44 percent

240. A normal distribution is one in which:

(A) The majority of scores are high.
(B) The majority of scores are low.
(C) All scores fall in the middle range.
(D) The majority of scores fall in the middle range.
(E) All scores are above the mean.

CHAPTER 13

Thought and Language

241. Because it has all the features commonly associated with the concept of a dog, a poodle is considered:

(A) An algorithm
(B) A heuristic
(C) A prototype
(D) A phoneme
(E) A concept

242. Which of the following is an example of functional fixedness?

(A) Using a blanket as a floor mat
(B) Not being able to solve a math problem because you are using the incorrect formula
(C) Replacing oil with applesauce when baking a cake
(D) Failing to use your keys to open a package when you can't find a pair of scissors
(E) Picking up a tangerine and calling it an orange

243. To become a chess or checkers champion one must use:

(A) Algorithms
(B) Heuristics
(C) Concepts
(D) Prototypes
(E) Morphemes

244. After watching the evening news, Khloe believes the newscast contains only tragic events like floods, earthquakes, and murders. When asked to think carefully about the newscast, she did recall many other events. This is an example of:

(A) Representative heuristic
(B) Availability heuristic
(C) Algorithm
(D) Functional fixedness
(E) Insight

245. Compared to divergent thinkers, convergent thinkers are more likely to:

(A) Think "outside the box" when problem solving
(B) Generate many different solutions when problem solving
(C) Choose to problem solve using an algorithm rather than a heuristic
(D) Use representative heuristics to problem solve
(E) Never allow functional fixedness to get in the way of problem solving

246. On her way to London, Janet was invited into the cockpit to meet the pilot, Alex. She was surprised to see that Alex was a woman. This is an example of:

(A) Confirmation bias
(B) Convergent thinking
(C) Insight
(D) Representative heuristic
(E) Availability heuristic

247. Phonemes are best defined as:

(A) The smallest meaningful combination of sounds in a language
(B) The basic sounds of consonants and vowels
(C) Something that specifies the meaning of words and phrases
(D) A set of rules that specify how we combine words to form meaningful sentences
(E) A special form of communication

248. Noam Chomsky's language theory included the idea that:

(A) Language development occurs between the ages of three and five.
(B) Children learn language through positive and negative reinforcement.
(C) Children make the same grammatical errors as their parents.
(D) Children model language development from those around them.
(E) Children have an innate mental grammar.

249. There is evidence to support the idea that there is an inborn tendency to absorb language. Which of the following psychologists would agree with this statement?

(A) Chomsky
(B) Whorf
(C) Skinner
(D) Saffron
(E) Sapir

250. Which of the following statements is *not* supported by the Whorf-Sapir linguistic relativity hypothesis?

(A) The language a person speaks determines the way a person thinks.
(B) If language lacks expression, the thought that corresponds will likely not occur.
(C) There is evidence to support that language development has inborn tendencies.
(D) If language affects our ability to store information, it should affect our thought process.
(E) To understand new vocabulary, it is easier to think about the relationship between language and thought.

251. Suppose you consider elderly people to be infirm and mentally slow. Every time you see elderly people in need of care or assistance, you take it as evidence of your belief, while ignoring the many cases of healthy, active elderly people. This is an example of:

(A) Representative heuristic
(B) Availability heuristic
(C) Prototype
(D) Confirmation bias
(E) Functional fixedness

252. Angie and Brad are looking to buy a new home. One criterion is a preference for a brick house. However, they would consider changing their minds and buying a wood house if it were located in a good school district and reasonably priced. In this case the attractive features offset the lack of brick exterior. This is an example of:

(A) Representative heuristic
(B) Compensatory model
(C) Noncompensatory model
(D) Availability heuristic
(E) Confirmation bias

253. Which of the following sentences best explains the idea of overregularization?

(A) Yesterday I goed to the store.
(B) I ain't going to the store.
(C) I no want to go to store.
(D) I want store.
(E) No store please.

254. Which of the following psychologists believes in the LAD, the language acquisition device?

(A) Whorf
(B) Seligman
(C) Kahneman
(D) Chomsky
(E) Sapir

255. When Mariah's mother drops her off at preschool, Mariah says only one word, "Mama." This is an example of:

(A) A heuristic
(B) Overgeneralization
(C) Framing
(D) Holophrase
(E) Phoneme

256. Which of the following statements best illustrates the concept of framing?

(A) A PSA for breast mammograms chooses to use the statement "you can die if you don't," rather than "this can save your life."
(B) Lily assumes her doctor named Chris is a male, when in fact she is female.
(C) An advertiser uses divergent thinking to come up with a commercial slogan.
(D) A person remembers items on a list depending on which order they appear in.
(E) A cigarette company puts beautiful women in its commercials.

257. Which of the following terms is an example of an innate sound program in the brain that involves making and processing sounds that will eventually be used to form words?

(A) Grammar
(B) Babbling
(C) Talking
(D) Sentences
(E) Morphemes

258. Rules of grammar can best be defined as:

(A) Acquiring language through four stages
(B) Phonemes and morphemes
(C) Problem solving using language
(D) Forming sentences that range from three to eight words
(E) Speaking in sentences that are stated in different ways but have the same meaning

259. Which of the following is *not* a good example of the ability to overcome functional fixedness?

(A) A potato is used as a temporary gas cap.
(B) A paper clip is used to make earrings.
(C) A glass is used as a paperweight.
(D) A credit card is used as a bookmark.
(E) A math formula is used to solve a math problem.

260. To develop a concept of an office, the definition theory states that one must:

(A) List all essential features of an office
(B) Construct an ideal office
(C) Look at the average office
(D) Visit various offices
(E) Transform a room into an office

261. Which of the following statements best describes an example of availability heuristic?

(A) After speaking in front of 200 people, Tim is no longer afraid of public speaking.
(B) Jane thinks all men will eventually cheat on her.
(C) Steven complains to his wife about work after a very bad day, but at the office party Steven's wife sees how much he enjoys what he does.
(D) Rob claims that when he is confronted with a problem, he likes to come up with one correct solution.
(E) After meeting a celebrity, Todd now wants to become an actor and eventually become famous.

262. Which of the following statements best defines information retrieval?

(A) Having memories of your 16th birthday party
(B) Thinking all dog owners are sensitive people
(C) Memorizing information that might be needed in an emergency
(D) Picking out the proper outfit to wear to a friend's housewarming party
(E) Writing a term paper

263. When solving an anagram one must try every possible combination of letters until the hidden word appears. This is an example of:

(A) A heuristic
(B) A concept
(C) A subgoal
(D) An image
(E) An algorithm

264. Which of the following terms is not an example of a problem-solving technique?

(A) Functional fixedness
(B) Trial and error
(C) Subgoals
(D) Brainstorming
(E) Heuristics

265. This problem-solving technique involves analyzing the difference between the current situation and the desired end, and then doing something to reduce that difference.

(A) Subgoals
(B) Means-end analysis
(C) Brainstorming
(D) Heuristic
(E) Algorithm

CHAPTER 14

Motivation

266. Motivation can best be defined as:

(A) An innate biological force that produces a fixed set of behaviors
(B) Various physiological and psychological factors that cause a person to act in a particular way
(C) A biological state in which an organism lacks something essential for survival
(D) The tendency or need for a body to stay in a balanced state
(E) Environmental factors that reward, reinforce, or encourage our behavior

267. Repulsion, curiosity, pugnacity, and humility are all examples of

(A) Needs
(B) Emotions
(C) Instincts
(D) Motivations
(E) Incentives

268. If a person does not eat for a period of time, it causes a need for food. This need produces a state of tension. The tension energizes the person to act in some way to find food, thereby returning the body to homeostasis. This is an example of:

(A) Intrinsic action pattern
(B) Sympathetic nervous system
(C) Extrinsic motivation
(D) Drive reduction theory
(E) Biological needs

269. A fixed action pattern is best illustrated by which of the following examples?

(A) Jackie's need to climb mountains
(B) Marlon's motivation to make a lot of money
(C) A baboon rising on hind feet when threatened
(D) A dog sitting by the window an hour before his owner comes home
(E) Michael's cat purring when she hears the can opener

270. Which of the following examples best illustrates an intrinsic motivation?

(A) Running a marathon to support breast cancer
(B) Rock climbing to win first prize
(C) Graduating with honors
(D) Trying out for the high school basketball team
(E) A teacher praising a student when she raises her hand

271. According to Maslow's hierarchy of needs, an adolescent who is beginning to form serious romantic relationships would be in what level?

(A) Level 1
(B) Level 2
(C) Level 3
(D) Level 4
(E) Level 5

272. According to Maslow's hierarchy of needs, an individual who quits his job and moves to Africa to do philanthropic work would be in what level?

(A) Level 1
(B) Level 2
(C) Level 3
(D) Level 4
(E) Level 5

273. Which of the following statements best illustrates Maslow's esteem needs?

(A) Moving to a safe community to raise your children
(B) Going to school to earn a master's degree in counseling
(C) Getting married to your high school sweetheart
(D) Donating a large sum of money to charity
(E) Going to the gym three days a week to improve your health

274. Which of the following factors signals hunger in our body?

(A) High levels of glucose
(B) Stimulation of the lateral hypothalamus
(C) Stimulation of the ventromedial hypothalamus
(D) High levels of cholecystokinin
(E) Stomach contractions

275. Homeostasis is best defined as:

(A) The physiological need to satisfy your hunger or thirst
(B) The body's tendency to maintain balance
(C) The arousal of the autonomic nervous system
(D) The release of the hormone serotonin
(E) The biological need for safety and security

276. If the ventromedial hypothalamus of a rat is destroyed:

(A) The rat will starve to death.
(B) The rat will only eat when it feels hungry.
(C) The rat will begin to feel full.
(D) The rat will become obese.
(E) The rat's blood glucose level will remain constant.

277. Which of the following statements best defines set point?

(A) It refers to how efficiently the body breaks food down.
(B) It refers to how quickly the body turns food into energy.
(C) It controls the body's metabolism.
(D) It plays a role in influencing appetite.
(E) It refers to a certain level of body fat that the body maintains.

278. An individual with a low metabolic rate is:

(A) More likely to have a fatter body
(B) Less likely to have a fatter body
(C) Less likely to store excess fuel
(D) More likely to eat more than someone with a high metabolic rate
(E) More likely to have an easier time losing weight

279. Which of the following is *not* an example of a psychological hunger factor?

(A) Social-cultural
(B) Learned associations
(C) Personality traits
(D) Peer pressure
(E) Nutrition

280. An individual's subjective experience and feeling of being either a male or female is referred to as:

(A) Gender roles
(B) Sexual orientation
(C) Gender identity
(D) Transgender
(E) Sex categories

281. By age five, children have acquired many of the complex thoughts and behaviors that accompany being male or female. This is best known as:

(A) Gender identity
(B) Gender roles
(C) Sexual identity
(D) Sexual cognition
(E) Gender cognition

282. Which of the following brain structures is most responsible for hunger and satiety, respectively?

(A) The ventromedial hypothalamus, the lateral hypothalamus
(B) The lateral hypothalamus, the ventromedial hypothalamus
(C) The amygdala, the hippocampus
(D) The hippocampus, the amygdala
(E) The cerebellum, the lateral hypothalamus

283. Which of the following statements is the core concept of Maslow's hierarchy of needs?

(A) Individuals who fail to reach self-actualization feel a sense of failure.
(B) Level 1 is the need for safety and security.
(C) Men are more concerned with safety needs and women are more concerned with esteem needs.
(D) Physiological needs must be met before an individual can attain self-actualization.
(E) An individual can skip levels 1, 2, and 3 and go directly to finding success at level 4.

284. A journalist chooses to go to Afghanistan to cover the war hoping to acquire the admiration of his peers and a promotion. Which of the following theories of motivation best explains this decision?

(A) Drive theory
(B) Incentive theory
(C) Fixed action pattern
(D) Socio-cognitive theory
(E) Motivation

285. Motivation starts with an individual's:

(A) Emotion
(B) Arousal
(C) Need
(D) Drive
(E) Incentive

CHAPTER 15

Emotion

286. Which of the following sequences is correct according to the James-Lange theory of emotion?

(A) Physiological changes, feel emotion, interpretation of emotion, observable behavior
(B) Physiological changes, interpretation of physiological change, feel emotion, observable behavior
(C) Feel emotion, physiological changes, interpretation of physiological change, observable behavior
(D) Brain interpretation, physiological changes, observable behavior
(E) Interpretation of stimuli, brain interpretation, physiological changes, observable behavior

287. What was the name of the theory on emotion that originated from the work of Charles Darwin?

(A) Facial feedback theory
(B) Cannon-Bard theory
(C) Cognitive-appraisal theory
(D) Affective-primacy theory
(E) Two-factor theory

288. What was one major criticism of the James-Lange theory on emotion?

(A) Emotions are usually associated with one specific physiological change in the body.
(B) Physiological changes do not vary in intensity.
(C) Different emotions are not necessarily associated with different patterns of physiological responses.
(D) Most emotions do not need a large amount of interpretation.
(E) Cognition has no direct affect on the physiological changes in the body.

289. Which of the following theories on emotion assumes that our interpretation or appraisal of a situation is the primary cause of emotion?

(A) Cannon-Bard theory
(B) Facial feedback theory
(C) James-Lange theory
(D) Schachter-Singer theory
(E) Peripheral theory

290. Which of the following statements best supports the Schachter-Singer theory of emotion?

(A) A friend walks up to you and tells you he saw someone back into your car and drive away—making you angry.
(B) You hear a loud noise, your heart starts to pound, and you know you are scared.
(C) You feel sad because you are crying.
(D) You know you are happy because you have been smiling all day.
(E) Your heart is racing but you are not sure why.

291. Unlike the cognitive-appraisal theory, the affective-primacy theory states:

(A) Physiological changes in the body happen simultaneously with the brain's interpretation of an event.
(B) The brain is entirely responsible for interpretations of any emotion one is having.
(C) Physiological changes in the body often determine the emotion one is feeling.
(D) In some situations, a person feels an emotion before having time to interpret the situation.
(E) Sometimes a person's interpretation of a situation is the primary cause of an emotion.

292. The six universal emotions specified that inherited facial patterns of expression are:

(A) Worried, sadness, anger, resentment, disgust, fear
(B) Happiness, sadness, anger, surprise, disgust, fear
(C) Happiness, excitement, anger, sadness, fear
(D) Confusion, happiness, sadness, anger, fear, disgust
(E) Happiness, sadness, resentment, anger, disgust, fear

293. Which of the following statements supports the results of the Ekman-Friesen experiment?

(A) Between five and seven months of age, infants show fear.
(B) It is difficult to communicate with people of different cultures.
(C) People show disgust for many different reasons.
(D) Babies smile due to modeling behavior.
(E) Children exhibit emotion differently than adults do.

294. Which statement best exemplifies the Yerkes-Dodson law?

(A) Many of Leo's friends think he is depressed due to his lack of any facial expressions.
(B) Josh has a look of disgust on his face after smelling the rotten milk.
(C) Linda spends hours playing a challenging video game because this activity arouses and motivates her.
(D) William's test anxiety helps him score higher on the exam.
(E) Jacob falls asleep in his physics class after being so bored.

295. Happiness includes all of the following *except*:

(A) Feeling a positive emotion
(B) Being satisfied with your life
(C) Not experiencing a negative emotion
(D) Having a high-paying job
(E) Both environmental and inherited factors

296. Three weeks after winning the lottery, Tanya gave birth to Sophia. Tanya claimed that winning the lottery was the most exciting thing to happen to her until she gave birth to her daughter. This is an example of:

(A) The adaptation level theory
(B) The rules of happiness theory
(C) The Yerkes-Dodson law
(D) The psycho-revolutionary theory
(E) The relative deprivation theory

297. Which statement best defines display rules?

(A) Specific inherited facial patterns or expressions are universal.
(B) People innately have a tendency to show affection in public.
(C) Many cultures do not allow public displays of emotion.
(D) Specific cultural norms regulate how much emotion we express socially.
(E) In some situations people feel an emotion before they have time to appraise the situation.

298. An interpretation or appraisal of a situation as having a positive or negative impact on your life resulting in a subjective feeling is called:

(A) The affective-primacy theory
(B) The James-Lange theory
(C) The Cannon-Bard theory
(D) The facial feedback theory
(E) The cognitive-appraisal theory

299. While sitting in a waiting room, a man next to you begins yelling and acting aggressively. Your heart begins beating fast. You interpret your environmental cues as the cause of your arousal. Which theory of emotion would support this explanation?

(A) The James-Lange theory
(B) The Schachter-Singer theory
(C) The affective-primacy theory
(D) All of the above
(E) None of the above

300. Which of the following theories of emotion support the idea that emotions and bodily responses occur simultaneously?

(A) The James-Lange theory
(B) The Schachter-Singer theory
(C) The Cannon-Bard theory
(D) The cognitive-appraisal theory
(E) The affective-primacy theory

301. Which of the following theories of emotion supports the importance of an individual's personal assessment of a situation?

(A) The cognitive-appraisal theory
(B) The Cannon-Bard theory
(C) The facial feedback theory
(D) The James-Lange theory
(E) The peripheral theory

302. "We feel sorry when we cry and afraid because we tremble." This quote is supported by which theory of emotion?

(A) The Cannon-Bard theory
(B) The James-Lange theory
(C) The Cannon-Lange theory
(D) The James-Bard theory
(E) The facial feedback theory

303. Larry really wants to buy his wife the diamond watch she always wanted for her birthday, but he knows he should be more conservative with his money. What type of conflict is he facing?

(A) Approach-approach
(B) Approach-avoidance
(C) Avoidance-avoidance
(D) Positive approach
(E) Negative approach

304. Which of the following examples best illustrates the concept of approach-approach conflict?

(A) Ariel must work at Bloomingdale's while in college.
(B) Sabrina is forced to call the home of one of her students because he is not doing his homework.
(C) Latoya has to choose between Princeton and Yale University.
(D) Wendy just got a promotion, but she now has to fire someone else.
(E) Randy works as a stand-up comedian, but he needs to make more money.

305. According to the Cannon-Bard theory of emotion, which part of the brain is vital in terms of physiological responses to emotion?

(A) The cerebellum
(B) The temporal lobe
(C) The frontal lobe
(D) The limbic system
(E) The left hemisphere

306. If we are about to jump out of an airplane for the first time, we tend to feel extreme fear along with low levels of elation. Later, when we decide to jump again, we experience more elation and less fear. This scenario is supported by which theory of emotion?

(A) The James-Lange theory
(B) The affective-primacy theory
(C) The opponent-process theory
(D) The Cannon-Bard theory
(E) None of the above

307. Emotional responses develop before complex thinking occurs. Which of the following psychologists would agree with this statement?

(A) Ekman
(B) Schachter
(C) Bard
(D) Lange
(E) Zajonc

308. Which area of the brain is extremely stimulated when an individual is feeling sad?

(A) Hypothalamus
(B) Thalamus
(C) Temporal lobe
(D) Parietal lobe
(E) Amygdala

309. Which example best illustrates the adaptation level theory?

(A) Michelle takes her mother's inheritance for granted.
(B) Regina has so much to do with so little free time to do it in.
(C) Natasha hired another assistant to help lessen her workload.
(D) Cathryn lost her brand-new wallet and bought a more expensive one.
(E) Alexis sold her engagement ring to send her son to college.

310. To achieve high performance on a simple task, the Yerkes-Dodson law recommends:

(A) High arousal
(B) Low arousal
(C) Medium arousal
(D) Extreme anxiety
(E) Moderate anxiety

CHAPTER 16

Developmental Psychology: Infancy and Childhood

311. Cross-sectional research differs from longitudinal research in that:

(A) Cross-sectional research studies the developmental changes of subjects who are of different ages.
(B) Cross-sectional research studies developmental changes using the same group of subjects over time as they grow older.
(C) Cross-sectional research is more reliable than developmental research.
(D) Cross-sectional research is too specific to the group of people being used for research.
(E) Cross-sectional research takes too much time to gather results.

312. Of the following sets of themes, which pair best represents the core emphasis of developmental psychology?

(A) Cross-sectional versus longitudinal and self-esteem versus self-doubt
(B) Individual versus shared and stability versus change
(C) Young versus old and stability versus change
(D) Individual versus shared and young versus old
(E) Stability versus change and self-esteem versus self-doubt

313. Which of the following reflexes is *not* a reflex infants enter the world equipped with?

(A) Sucking
(B) Swallowing
(C) Stepping
(D) Rooting
(E) Licking

314. Temperament is best defined as:
- (A) Personality traits inherited from biological parents
- (B) Learned behavioral tendencies of a young child
- (C) Physical and emotional characteristics of a newborn child and young infant
- (D) Psychological and physiological personality traits a young child models from his or her environment
- (E) Emotional traits that infants outgrow by the time they turn two years old

315. Research has determined that, between the ages of 6 and 12 months, all babies have acquired:
- (A) Three-dimensional dreaming
- (B) The ability to walk
- (C) The ability to talk
- (D) Depth perception
- (E) Potty-training abilities

316. Motor development in babies develops in a proximodistal fashion. This is best described as:
- (A) From nearest to the center of the body to the farthest from the center
- (B) From the top of the head to the bottom of the feet
- (C) From the farthest from the center to the nearest to the center
- (D) From the bottom of the body to the top of the body
- (E) From the left of the body to the right of the body

317. Which of the following statements best defines maturation?
- (A) It is directly based on social cognitive learning.
- (B) It is the basis for all physiological and psychological development.
- (C) It is an automatic biological development of the body and nervous system that naturally unfolds over time.
- (D) It does not take place in all human beings.
- (E) It is directly associated with genetic links.

318. According to Jean Piaget, at what stages of development are children able to grasp the concepts of object permanence and conservation, respectively?
- (A) Formal operational; preoperational
- (B) Concrete operational; formal operational
- (C) Concrete operational; sensorimotor
- (D) Sensorimotor; preoperational
- (E) Sensorimotor; concrete operational

319. Jean Piaget defined egocentrism as:

(A) The belief that young adults don't listen to their parents
(B) The idea that preschool children cannot see things from another's point of view
(C) The understanding that young children cannot learn outside of a structured classroom
(D) The idea that young children are selfish and grow out of it over time
(E) The belief that children cannot do more than one task at a time

320. According to Jean Piaget, what type of learning do individuals acquire during the formal operational stage?

(A) Abstract thought
(B) Symbolism
(C) Memorization skills
(D) Visual learning
(E) Auditory learning

321. An awareness that objects continue to exist when out of sight is called:

(A) Mental images
(B) Sensory-motor
(C) Object permanence
(D) Object understanding
(E) Conservation

322. According to Jean Piaget, children understand the concept of symbolism during which stage of development?

(A) Sensory-motor
(B) Preoperational
(C) Concrete operational
(D) Formal operational
(E) Operational

323. One major difference between assimilation and accommodation is that assimilation:

(A) Is a process by which children use old methods to deal with new situations
(B) Is a process by which children change their thought process to meet the needs of their world
(C) Is a process by which children gain an understanding of the world around them
(D) Is a process by which individuals shape their lives based on learned observations
(E) Is a process by which individuals begin using hypothetical thinking skills

324. According to Lawrence Kohlberg, during the preconventional stage of moral development children tend to:

(A) Use abstract thoughts or principles to determine their behavior
(B) Make behavioral decisions based on legal issues
(C) Understand morality based on customs or values
(D) Interpret behavior in terms of concrete consequences
(E) Define good behavior as that which pleases other people

325. During a discussion in class regarding cheating in school, a student argues, "Cheating is wrong; it is important to follow rules." Lawrence Kohlberg would say this student is in what stage of moral development?

(A) Preconventional
(B) Conventional
(C) Postconventional
(D) Nonconventional
(E) Advanced conventional

326. As a preschooler, Emma has developed a number of cognitive and social skills that she will use to assume responsibility. According to Erik Erikson, what stage of psychosocial development is Emma in?

(A) Trust versus mistrust
(B) Autonomy versus self-doubt
(C) Initiative versus guilt
(D) Industry versus inferiority
(E) Identity versus role confusion

327. When Daniel begins walking, talking, and exploring, he is bound to get into conflict with his parents. If his parents punish his explorations, Daniel may develop a feeling that independence is bad. According to Erik Erikson, what stage of psychosocial development would this occur in?

(A) Identity versus role confusion
(B) Industry versus inferiority
(C) Initiative versus guilt
(D) Autonomy versus self-doubt
(E) Trust versus mistrust

328. According to Sigmund Freud, what is the correct order of the five psychosexual stages of development?

(A) Oral, anal, phallic, early, genital
(B) Oral, anal, phallic, latency, genital
(C) Anal, phallic, latency, genital, oral
(D) Genital, oral, latency, phallic, anal
(E) Phallic, anal, oral, latency, genital

329. If individuals successfully solve their problems during each stage of life, they will develop good social traits. If they do not, their problem-solving skills will be hindered, causing new problems at the next stage. Which psychologist(s) would agree with this statement?

(A) Freud
(B) Piaget
(C) Erikson
(D) A and B
(E) A and C

330. Monica is extremely neat and orderly. She cannot stand it when people touch things on her desk. She also has a problem lending money to even her closest friends. Freud would say she is stuck in what psychosexual stage?

(A) Oral
(B) Anal
(C) Phallic
(D) Latency
(E) Genital

331. Jenna is extremely sarcastic. She uses this to cover up her low self-esteem. Freud would say she is stuck in which psychosexual stage?

(A) Oral
(B) Anal
(C) Phallic
(D) Latency
(E) Genital

332. If a child believes stealing in order to save a life is OK because life is even more important than following the law, this child would be in what stage of moral development?

(A) Level one: preconventional
(B) Level two: conventional
(C) Level three: postconventional
(D) Level four: operational
(E) Level five: formal operational

333. Which of the following statements is a major criticism of Jean Piaget's work with cognitive development?

(A) Piaget failed to include clear age differences for his stages.
(B) Piaget placed too much emphasis on cognitive differences between young children and adolescents.
(C) Piaget often overestimated the cognitive abilities of children.
(D) Piaget often underestimated the cognitive abilities of children.
(E) Piaget gave little credit to other psychologists who helped him develop his theory.

334. The rooting reflex is an infant's tendency to:

(A) Throw legs up in the air
(B) Wave arms when startled
(C) Open mouth and turn head when touched on the cheek
(D) Follow a moving object with eyes
(E) Grasp nearby objects

335. Harry Harlow's experiment with monkeys and surrogate mothers emphasized the importance of:

(A) Satisfying hunger
(B) Body temperature
(C) Fulfilling needs
(D) Intrinsic motivation
(E) Contact

CHAPTER 17

Developmental Psychology: Adolescence and Adulthood

336. When adolescents were asked about their major concerns for their future, top answers on their lists were getting married, having friends, getting a job, and doing well in school. Each of these concerns involves the ability to understand abstract thought and concepts. According to Jean Piaget, what stage of cognitive learning is this?

(A) Sensorimotor
(B) Preoperational
(C) Operational
(D) Formal operational
(E) Postoperational

337. While at her friend's party, Angelica begins to feel self-conscious because she assumes everyone is staring at her. According to David Elkind, what adolescent belief is Angelica feeling?

(A) Imaginary audience
(B) Personal fable
(C) Awkwardness
(D) Insecure attachment
(E) Imaginary persona

338. Which of the following examples best illustrates a personal fable?

(A) Talia feels insecure when she is making her presentation in front of her class.
(B) Lola feels as though no one else could possibly be so much in love as she is.
(C) Dina lies to her parents about going to her boyfriend's birthday party.
(D) Alexa is no longer interested in her schoolwork; all she wants to do is hang out with her friends.
(E) Joanna falls into a severe depression when her boyfriend breaks up with her.

339. Authoritative parents can best be defined as:

(A) Parents who befriend their children and do not use discipline
(B) Parents who are less controlling and behave with a more accepting attitude
(C) Parents who try to control the behavior of their children in accordance with a set standard of conduct
(D) Supportive parents who discuss their rules and policies with their children
(E) Parents who command obedience and teach their values with little communication

340. According to Erik Erikson, what is one major conflict teenagers deal with during the identity versus role confusion stage of psychosocial development?

(A) Finding a more purposeful life as an adult
(B) Achieving personal satisfaction
(C) Reflecting on previous life challenges
(D) Finding intimacy by developing loving relationships
(E) Achieving generativity through family relationships

341. According to Robert Sternberg, what are the three components of love?

(A) Passion, romance, attraction
(B) Commitment, intimacy, companionship
(C) Passion, intimacy, commitment
(D) Intimacy, trust, attraction
(E) Intimacy, companionship, attraction

342. Carol Gilligan believed moral decision making is dependent primarily on which of the following?

(A) Age
(B) Culture
(C) Religion
(D) Gender
(E) Nationality

343. Which of the following parenting styles results in the most socially responsible adults?

(A) Authoritarian
(B) Authoritative
(C) Permissive
(D) Autocratic
(E) Sensitive

344. A failure to develop a consistent identity results in:

(A) Role confusion
(B) Inferiority
(C) Insecurity
(D) Stagnation
(E) Social isolation

345. According to Erikson, teachers, friends, and other people outside of the home first become important in shaping attitudes of a child during what psychosocial stage?

(A) Autonomy versus self-doubt
(B) Initiative versus guilt
(C) Industry versus inferiority
(D) Integrity versus despair
(E) Trust versus mistrust

346. Daniel Levinson studied:

(A) Child development
(B) Adolescent behavior
(C) Death and dying
(D) Male adult psychosocial stages
(E) Female adult psychosocial stages

347. According to Erikson, a child who is learning the importance of academic success in school based on receiving a report card is in what psychosocial stage?

(A) Industry versus inferiority
(B) Generativity versus stagnation
(C) Identity versus role confusion
(D) Initiative versus guilt
(E) Integrity versus despair

348. I am in my early fifties. If I do not reach out to others, especially young people, Erik Erikson says I will experience:

(A) Shame
(B) Depression
(C) Isolation
(D) Stagnation
(E) Despair

349. According to Lawrence Kohlberg, behavior directed by self-accepted moral principles is an example of what stage of moral development?

(A) Preconventional
(B) Conventional
(C) Postconventional
(D) Nonconventional
(E) Unconventional

350. According to Erik Erikson, as a young adult you are most interested in developing:

(A) Initiative
(B) Integrity
(C) Generativity
(D) Trust
(E) Intimacy

351. Which group of stages from Erikson, Kohlberg, and Levinson identify the same phase of life?

(A) Identity, conventional, age 50 crisis
(B) Generativity, postconventional, age 50 crisis
(C) Generativity, preconventional, midlife transition
(D) Intimacy, preconventional, midlife transition
(E) Initiative, conventional, age 30 crisis

352. According to Freud adolescents are in what psychosexual stage?

(A) Oral
(B) Anal
(C) Phallic
(D) Latency
(E) Genital

353. Which three psychologists focused their work on adolescent development?

(A) Freud, Kohlberg, Gilligan
(B) Gilligan, Erikson, Havighurst
(C) Havighurst, Elkind, Marcia
(D) Marcia, Levinson, Elkind
(E) Elkind, Freud, Piaget

354. As children begin their elementary school years, they enter Erikson's stage of:

(A) Trust versus mistrust
(B) Autonomy versus doubt
(C) Initiative versus guilt
(D) Industry versus inferiority
(E) Identity versus role confusion

355. Robert Havighurst believed adolescents must:

(A) Complete a series of tasks
(B) Fall in love
(C) Graduate college
(D) Get along with their parents
(E) Find a summer job

CHAPTER 18

Developmental Psychology: Death and Dying

356. Claire just celebrated her 90th birthday with her family and close friends. According to Erik Erikson, she has probably achieved:

(A) Isolation
(B) Integrity
(C) Despair
(D) Autonomy
(E) Stagnation

357. Which is the correct order of the five stages of dealing with death or loss?

(A) Denial, anger, bargaining, depression, acceptance
(B) Anger, denial, bargaining, depression, acceptance
(C) Bargaining, anger, denial, depression, acceptance
(D) Depression, bargaining, anger, denial, acceptance
(E) Depression, anger, denial, bargaining, acceptance

358. Which of the following psychologists formulated a stage theory addressing our encounters with grief?

(A) Sigmund Freud
(B) Erik Erikson
(C) Elisabeth Kubler-Ross
(D) Carol Gilligan
(E) Lawrence Kohlberg

359. In late adulthood, individuals experience a decrease in which of the following?

(A) Sexual desire
(B) Cognitive abilities
(C) Creativity
(D) Intellect
(E) Compassion for others

360. Ethel, who is 80 years old, lost her husband last year, and her children hardly ever come to visit. She looks back on her life with a lot of regret. According to Erik Erikson she is experiencing:

(A) Stagnation
(B) Depression
(C) Regression
(D) Despair
(E) Isolation

CHAPTER 19

Freudian Psychology

361. Freud's psychodynamic theory of personality emphasizes:

(A) The importance of early childhood experiences
(B) The importance of sibling rivalries
(C) The role genetics plays in personality development
(D) The nature-nurture debate
(E) The conscious thought process only

362. To explain why we do things that we cannot explain, Freud used the concept of:

(A) Conscious forces
(B) Subconscious tendencies
(C) Unconscious motivation
(D) Preconscious motivation
(E) Conscious association

363. The Freudian technique in which clients are encouraged to talk about any thoughts that enter their mind to help with uncensored talk is called:

(A) Unconscious motivation
(B) Free association
(C) Free analysis
(D) Freudian interpretation
(E) Psychodynamic theory

364. Freud believed the mental process must have a source of energy called:

(A) Ego
(B) Superego
(C) Id
(D) Conscious
(E) Unconscious

365. As children learn they must follow rules and regulations in satisfying their wishes, they develop:

(A) A superego
(B) An id
(C) An ego
(D) A preconscious
(E) An unconscious

366. As infants discover that parents put restrictions on satisfying their wishes, infants learn to control their wishes. According to Freud they do this through the development of:

(A) An id
(B) A superego
(C) An ego
(D) A conscious
(E) A subconscious

367. Which of the following examples best illustrates the pleasure principle?

(A) A student takes pleasure in reporting a fellow classmate for cheating.
(B) A new mother breastfeeds her infant.
(C) A corporate executive takes a vacation after working extremely hard the past month.
(D) A spoiled child acts out by throwing his toys at the wall when he doesn't get the Christmas gift he wanted.
(E) A mother and father fight about whether their son should have the privilege of staying out late to attend a party.

368. A defense mechanism is best defined by Freud as:

(A) A systematic process used to avoid confrontation
(B) A thought process that operates at an unconscious level to help an individual reduce anxiety
(C) The creation of acceptable excuses for unacceptable behavior
(D) The transfer of feelings from the unconscious to the conscious
(E) A thought process by which forbidden desires are acknowledged

369. Todd has had a crush on Donna for the past year, but he does not have the courage to ask her out. He is frustrated with himself and begins taking a kickboxing class at his local gym. This scenario best illustrates which defense mechanism?

(A) Displacement
(B) Projection
(C) Reaction formation
(D) Rationalization
(E) Sublimation

370. Which of the following statements best illustrates rationalization?

(A) Jay fails his math class and blames it on his teacher not liking him.
(B) After fighting with her best friend, Annie starts an argument with her mother.
(C) Janie feels so guilty about cheating, she confesses to her teacher.
(D) Conner is a heavy smoker but disregards all the evidence that says smoking can kill you.
(E) Jarred doesn't want to believe that his pastor could have molested his younger brother.

371. Tom is still in love with his girlfriend, who broke up with him last week, but he acts as if he doesn't care and is actually happy to be rid of her. This is an example of which of the following defense mechanisms?

(A) Regression
(B) Projection
(C) Sublimation
(D) Displacement
(E) Reaction formation

372. According to Freud, what is the preconscious?

(A) Another name for conscious
(B) The opposing force for the unconscious
(C) The part of the mind that is right below the conscious surface
(D) The part of the mind that works directly with the id
(E) The part of the unconscious that does not hold repressed desires

373. According to Freud, in what stage of psychosexual development does the Oedipus complex take place?

(A) Oral
(B) Anal
(C) Latency
(D) Phallic
(E) Genital

374. The female version of the Oedipus complex is called

(A) Victoria complex
(B) Isabella complex
(C) Pleasure complex
(D) Electra complex
(E) Octavia complex

375. According to Freud's psychosexual theory of development, a man's repression of sexual urges is a result of which of the following?

(A) Fixation in the latency stage
(B) Fixation in the oral stage
(C) Fixation in the anal stage
(D) Fixation in the genital stage
(E) Fixation in the phallic stage

376. One major criticism of Freudian psychoanalytic theory is that it:

(A) Focuses too much attention on sexual conflicts and fixations
(B) Assumes all behaviors are learned during childhood
(C) Is too pessimistic about the future of humanity
(D) Focuses too much attention on the id and not enough on the ego
(E) Gives too much power to conscious behavior

377. A three-year-old boy is rejecting his father and only wants to be around his mother. Freud would theorize the child is going through which phase?

(A) Electra complex
(B) Pleasure principle
(C) Oedipus complex
(D) Reality principle
(E) Latency period

378. Grace realizes she got back an extra hundred dollars from the bank teller. She has to decide whether or not she should return to the bank and inform the bank teller of the mistake. Grace is currently in conflict between her:

(A) Conscious and unconscious
(B) Id and superego
(C) Ego and superego
(D) Preconscious and unconscious
(E) Id and conscious

379. A fixation in the oral stage will include all of the following behaviors *except*:

(A) Overeating
(B) Low self-esteem
(C) Sarcasm
(D) Self-consciousness
(E) Aggressiveness

380. James has been divorced twice. Now anytime he even goes out on a date with women, they tell him he is very misogynistic. James could be fixated in what psychosexual stage of development?

(A) Oral
(B) Anal
(C) Phallic
(D) Latency
(E) Genital

Personality Psychology

381. The "anima," "animus," "persona," and "shadow" are all:

(A) Archetypes in the collective unconscious according to Carl Jung
(B) Parts of the drive for superiority according to Alfred Adler
(C) Components of Karen Horney's beliefs on neurotic needs
(D) Terms used by Sigmund Freud to explain the Oedipus complex
(E) Roles encouraged by neo-Freudians

382. Which theory of personality emphasizes the value and importance of unconditional positive regard with regard to relationships?

(A) Psychoanalytic psychology
(B) Humanistic psychology
(C) Cognitive psychology
(D) Developmental psychology
(E) Behavioral psychology

383. The "Big Five" personality characteristics are:

(A) Emotionality, extroversion, openness, neuroticism, and agreeableness
(B) Anxiety, extroversion, agreeableness, neuroticism, and sociability
(C) Outgoing, conscientiousness, extroversion, agreeableness, and neuroticism
(D) Openness, conscientiousness, extroversion, agreeableness, and neuroticism
(E) Extroversion, neuroticism, anxiety, agreeableness, and openness

384. Research shows that individuals with a type A personality are more prone to:

(A) Extroversion
(B) Cardiac health problems
(C) Poverty
(D) Sexual dysfunction
(E) Psychoticism

385. Which of the following statements is a good example of a Jungian archetype?

(A) Owen, who is 37, still wants to please his domineering mother.
(B) Erica does not want anyone to know she uses food stamps.
(C) George runs for class president because he wants his classmates to believe he is a confident person.
(D) Tanya consciously strives to become the best golf player on her team.
(E) Joan, who is haunted by her memories of child abuse, seeks help by going to a psychotherapist.

386. Which of the following tests is an example of a projective test, consisting of a set of ambiguous pictures about which people are asked to tell a story?

(A) MMPI-2
(B) Rorschach
(C) LSAT
(D) TAT
(E) ASW

387. Which of the following terms does *not* describe the assumption behind Carl Rogers's self theory?

(A) Unconditional positive regard
(B) Congruency
(C) Self-actualization
(D) Empathic understanding
(E) Extraversion

388. According to Carl Rogers, a client's personality is determined by measuring the difference between:

(A) Introversion and extraversion
(B) Ideal self and real self
(C) Self-efficacy and self-esteem
(D) Persona and shadow
(E) Self-actualization and esteem needs

389. According to Albert Bandura, self-efficacy is best described as:

(A) The way in which an individual views his or her self-worth
(B) A voluntary decision to postpone a personal reward until a specific task is completed
(C) An individual's personal beliefs regarding how capable he or she is in controlling events and completing tasks
(D) An individual's social, political, and cultural views on issues that influence his or her learning potential
(E) An individual's beliefs about how much control he or she has over choices he or she has and decisions he or she makes

390. Ted believes that when he graduates depends primarily on his motivation and determination. This thought process is called:

(A) Self-efficacy
(B) Self-actualization
(C) Social cognition
(D) Internal locus of control
(E) External locus of control

391. Raymond Cattell claimed that 35 basic traits could describe all differences among personalities. He called these ________________ traits.

(A) External
(B) Internal
(C) Social
(D) Source
(E) Diverse

392. The trait theory can best be defined as:

(A) The analysis of how much personality or behavioral traits are influenced by genetics
(B) The analysis of the structure of personality by classifying similarities and differences in personality characteristics
(C) A factor analysis that studies common personality characteristics
(D) The organization of personality traits using specific categories to describe all characteristics
(E) Grouping individual behaviors based on interactions between particular personality characteristics

393. A true-false self-report questionnaire that describes a wide range of normal and abnormal behaviors is called:

(A) Thematic Apperception Test
(B) Validity Test
(C) Rorschach Test
(D) Objective Personality Test
(E) Minnesota Multiphasic Personality Inventory

394. Complete the following statement: The ________________ theory minimized the role of the unconscious.

(A) Humanistic
(B) Trait
(C) Psychoanalytic
(D) Behaviorist
(E) Functionalist

395. According to Carl Jung, the collective unconscious consists of:

(A) Inherent tendencies to help people develop their true potential
(B) Mental processes of which we are unaware but which automatically influence our thought patterns
(C) Ancient memories and symbols that are passed down from birth and shared by all people in all cultures
(D) Forces that influence our behavior
(E) Biological drives shared by all people in all cultures

396. Alfred Adler proposed that humans are motivated by:

(A) Conscious drives
(B) Neurotic needs
(C) Empathic understanding
(D) Social urges
(E) Intrinsic motivation

397. Which of the following neo-Freudians believed that the major influence on personality development is found in the child-parent social interaction?

(A) Adler
(B) Horney
(C) Jung
(D) Rogers
(E) Bandura

398. According to Alfred Adler, fictional finalism is best defined as:

(A) The belief that people live by many ideals that have no relation to reality
(B) The desire people have to do good for their community
(C) An individual's need to be in complete control over his or her life
(D) The desire for power that all human beings innately struggle with
(E) The social urges all people are motivated by and the unique way individuals deal with those urges

399. Neo-Freudians agree with Freud on all of the following basic ideas *except*:

(A) Importance of the unconscious
(B) The division of the mind
(C) The use of defense mechanisms
(D) The importance of sexual drives and conflicts
(E) The protection of the ego

400. The importance of our capacity for personal growth, development of our potential, and freedom to choose our destiny is the emphasis of which psychological theory?

(A) Psychoanalytic psychology
(B) Existentialism
(C) Behaviorism
(D) Humanism
(E) Cognitive psychology

CHAPTER 21

Stress and Coping

401. Stress is *best* defined as:

(A) A subjective evaluation of a situation that we believe to be overwhelming
(B) A threatening feeling that comes when we interpret a situation as more than our psychological or physiological resources can handle
(C) A potentially harmful situation from which we can potentially sustain some harm or damage
(D) A situation that we see as a challenge to our psyche
(E) A measure of how much we can handle a potentially threatening situation

402. Lamar was asked to give blood. He has a terrible fear of doing so. He automatically thinks this will have negative effects on his well-being. This is an example of what type of appraisal?

(A) Harm/loss
(B) Challenge
(C) Threat
(D) Stress
(E) Negative

403. Which of the following statements is true regarding the fight-flight response?

(A) It can be triggered by physical stimuli that threaten our survival.
(B) It directs a great source of energy from the brain to the muscles.
(C) It calms the body down after the response to a stress stimuli has occurred.
(D) It stimulates the thyroid gland to release a stress hormone called adrenaline.
(E) It automatically reduces physiological stress triggers by slowing down the heart rate.

404. Physical symptoms such as headaches, muscle pain, and stomach problems brought on by psychological factors like worry and tension are called:

(A) Resistance symptoms
(B) Prolonged stress symptoms
(C) Psychological symptoms
(D) Psychosomatic symptoms
(E) Appraisal symptoms

405. Stress appraisal stimulates which part of the brain?

(A) Thalamus
(B) Hypothalamus
(C) Amygdala
(D) Cerebrum
(E) Medulla

406. When the adrenal medulla is activated by the sympathetic nervous system, ________________ is secreted.

(A) Epinephrine
(B) Dopamine
(C) Serotonin
(D) Acetylcholine
(E) Glycogen

407. What are the three stages of the general adaptation syndrome (GAS)?

(A) Alarm, fight, relaxation
(B) Alarm, control, exhaustion
(C) Resistance, alarm, homeostasis
(D) Alarm, resistance, exhaustion
(E) Resistance, exhaustion, relaxation

408. Which of the following examples best illustrates frustration?

(A) A basketball coach loses his temper when his team loses a game they should have won.
(B) Two wolves fight to become the leader of the pack.
(C) A child starts crying when his mother says good-bye to him in preschool.
(D) A spider eats a fly.
(E) A farmer kills a chicken to eat for dinner.

409. When we balance the demands of a potentially stressful situation with our ability to meet these demands, it is called:

(A) Secondary appraisal
(B) Threat appraisal
(C) Harm/loss appraisal
(D) Challenge appraisal
(E) Primary appraisal

410. Eva's professor keeps telling her how the tests and quizzes she takes in his class are opportunities to demonstrate her understanding of the material. Eva's professor is attempting to elicit what kind of appraisal?

(A) Harm/loss
(B) Threat
(C) Challenge
(D) Primary
(E) Secondary

411. What effect do harm/loss appraisals have that challenge appraisals do not have?

(A) Lower physiological arousal
(B) Higher levels of negative emotions
(C) More psychological stimulation
(D) A triggering of physiological arousal
(E) Increased activity of the parasympathetic nervous system

412. In what stage of the general adaptation syndrome is there a breakdown to internal organs and a weakening of the immune system?

(A) Alarm
(B) Resistance
(C) Exhaustion
(D) Relaxation
(E) Negative

413. Just before her solo at her chorus concert, Charlene's heart begins to race and her face becomes flushed. According to Hans Selye, Charlene is in what stage of stress?

(A) Alarm
(B) Resistance
(C) Exhaustion
(D) Primary
(E) Psychosomatic

414. Which of the following is *not* an example of a major source of stress?

(A) Hassles
(B) Change
(C) Pressure
(D) Frustration
(E) Fear

415. Richard Lazarus's theory on stress emphasizes which of the following as the first step in experiencing stress?

(A) Fear
(B) Threat
(C) Flight
(D) Appraisal
(E) Threat

CHAPTER 22

Disorders

416. A mental disorder is generally defined as:

(A) Not knowing the difference between right and wrong
(B) A prolonged problem that interferes with an individual's ability to cope in society
(C) An anxiety disorder with dangers of hurting oneself
(D) A long-term problem that can only be cured with medication
(E) A long-term problem that cannot be treated with medication

417. Lee is unable to tell the difference between right and wrong in any aspect of his life. This statement is describing which type of abnormal behavior?

(A) Depression
(B) Maladaptive
(C) Insanity
(D) Anxiety
(E) Psychotic

418. The learning perspective states that the main cause of mental disorders is:

(A) Reinforcement of maladaptive behavior learned through experience
(B) Irrational thought processes
(C) Internal conflict from one's childhood
(D) Low self-esteem
(E) Chemical imbalance in the brain

419. DSM-IV was designed to help with which of the following?

(A) Identifying psychological disorders
(B) Identifying the causes of psychological disorders
(C) Classifying psychological disorders
(D) Listing venues where individuals can diagnose their disorder
(E) Distinguishing between sanity and insanity

420. A somatoform disorder can best be defined as:

(A) Disorder in which hallucinations occur often
(B) Disorder in which an individual experiences extreme anxiety
(C) Disorder in which symptoms are completely made up by the individual
(D) Disorder in which symptoms are produced by psychological factors
(E) Disorder in which an individual has delusional thoughts

421. Which of the following examples best illustrates a person with obsessive-compulsive disorder (OCD)?

(A) Steven hyperventilates whenever he is in an elevator.
(B) Shelly complains constantly about feeling sick and goes to many doctors.
(C) Bari is extremely anxious and panics every time she gets on an airplane.
(D) Blake wanders around town in a daze, not sure how she got there.
(E) Adam must lock his door 10 times before he leaves for work every morning.

422. A soldier experiences sudden blindness after returning from battle. He would most likely be diagnosed with which of the following disorders?

(A) Conversion disorder
(B) Dissociative disorder
(C) Bipolar disorder
(D) Hypochondriac
(E) A phobic disorder

423. Which of the following disorders is *not* an anxiety disorder?

(A) Phobias
(B) Panic
(C) Hypochondriasis
(D) Obsessive-compulsive
(E) Post-traumatic stress

424. This disorder is characterized by irritability, difficulty concentrating, and inability to control one's worry.

(A) Phobias
(B) Generalized anxiety
(C) Obsessive-compulsive
(D) Bipolar
(E) Hypochondriasis

425. Fran was sitting on the bus when she suddenly felt overwhelmed. Her heart started racing, her legs began to feel weak, and her body trembled. She thought she was losing her mind. Fran's symptoms indicate she has:

(A) Bipolar disorder
(B) Panic disorder
(C) Schizophrenia
(D) Obsessive-compulsive disorder
(E) Personality disorder

426. Agoraphobia is the fear of:

(A) Heights
(B) Spiders
(C) The dark
(D) Being in places with no escape
(E) Speaking in public

427. Which of the following symptoms is *not* a symptom of obsessive-compulsive disorder?

(A) Irrational thoughts
(B) Impulsive behavior
(C) Uncontrollable images
(D) Severe depression
(E) Ritualized behavior

428. Individuals who have reported paralysis of a limb, blindness, or seizures with no physical or neurological damage are most likely suffering from:

(A) A conversion disorder
(B) A panic disorder
(C) Post-traumatic stress disorder
(D) Hypochondriasis
(E) Bipolar disorder

429. Axis II of the DSM-IV refers to which of the following?

(A) Mood disorders
(B) Personality disorders
(C) Anxiety disorders
(D) Schizophrenia
(E) General medical conditions

430. Which of the following disorders has psychological stressors translating into physical symptoms?

(A) Anxiety
(B) Adjustment
(C) Affective
(D) Somatoform
(E) Psychotic

431. Data suggests that the most common mental disorder is:

(A) Substance abuse
(B) Mood disorders
(C) Personality disorders
(D) Somatoform disorders
(E) Psychosexual disorders

432. Which of the following treatments is most often used to help clients who suffer from obsessive-compulsive disorder?

(A) Avoidance therapy
(B) Psychoanalysis
(C) Exposure therapy
(D) Biochemical treatment
(E) Cognitive therapy

433. A list of criteria and symptoms about the onset, severity, and duration of mental disorders is located in which axis of the DSM-IV?

(A) Axis I
(B) Axis II
(C) Axis III
(D) Axis IV
(E) Axis V

434. The theory that states that mental disorders develop when a biological predisposition to the disorder is set off by stressful circumstances is:

(A) Cognitive-behavioral model
(B) Psychoanalytic model
(C) Diathesis-stress model
(D) Biochemical model
(E) Developmental model

435. Gender-identity disorders involve:

(A) The use of unconventional sexual tendencies
(B) The desire to dress like individuals of the opposite sex
(C) Homosexual tendencies
(D) The rejection of one's biological gender
(E) The rejection of gender-related stereotypes

CHAPTER 23

Mood Disorders and Schizophrenia

436. Which of the following disorders does *not* fall under a mood disorder?

(A) Dysthymic disorder
(B) Bipolar disorder
(C) Major depression
(D) Cyclothymic disorder
(E) Schizophrenia

437. Lilly is now 35 years old. She just started therapy because she feels "down in the dumps." While in therapy she realizes she has felt this way most of her life. She is most likely suffering from:

(A) Major depression
(B) Bipolar disorder
(C) Dysthymic disorder
(D) Generalized anxiety disorder
(E) Antisocial personality disorder

438. Antidepressant drugs work mainly because they raise the level of a single neurotransmitter called:

(A) Dopamine
(B) Epinephrine
(C) Norepinephrine
(D) Serotonin
(E) Glycogen

439. Which of the following characteristics in *not* a symptom of a personality disorder?

(A) Major depression
(B) Inflexibility
(C) Maladaptive traits
(D) Impaired functioning
(E) Great social and personal distress

440. Jeff has total disregard for the rights or properties of others. He steals all the time from just about anyone. He randomly harasses people. He has consistently destroyed his neighbor's property. Last month he was arrested for kidnapping. While in jail he continues to lie and have little remorse for his actions. Jeff is suffering from what mental disorder?

(A) Major depression
(B) Psychopath
(C) Schizoid personality disorder
(D) Dependent personality disorder
(E) Paranoid personality disorder

441. Which of the following symptoms best illustrates schizoid personality disorder?

(A) Disregard for the rights of others, feeling little to no remorse for bad behavior
(B) Submissive behavior, excessive need to be taken care of
(C) Acute discomfort in close relationships, distorted thinking, and eccentric behavior
(D) Intense desire to be orderly, having total control over others
(E) Excessively emotional and delusional, accompanied by a strong need for attention

442. Which of the following characterizes paranoid personality disorder?

(A) Unstable moods
(B) Lack of social relationships
(C) Lack of conscience
(D) Inaccurate sense of self-worth
(E) Extreme suspiciousness and mistrust of other people

443. Early childhood sexual or physical abuse is a common feature among people suffering from:

(A) Somatoform disorder
(B) Dissociative identity disorder
(C) Bipolar disorder
(D) Major depression
(E) Schizophrenia

444. From the time he was a young child, Scott has had no problem lying to authority figures. As an adult he considers himself good with the ladies. He has little remorse for his maladaptive behavior. Scott would most likely be diagnosed with:

(A) Antisocial personality disorder
(B) Paranoid personality disorder
(C) Narcissistic personality disorder
(D) Schizoid personality disorder
(E) Schizophrenia

445. Pricilla spent the last four weeks in bed. Without telling her friends or family she bought a three-thousand-dollar plane ticket to Europe. She took most of her savings with her to go on a major shopping spree when she gets there. Pricilla is most likely suffering from:

(A) Narcissistic personality disorder
(B) Major depression
(C) Schizoid personality disorder
(D) Bipolar disorder
(E) Dysthymic disorder

446. Excessive dopamine is to ________________ as too little dopamine is to ________________.

(A) Parkinson's disease, schizophrenia
(B) Schizophrenia, Parkinson's disease
(C) Antisocial personality disorder, schizoid personality disorder
(D) Depression, schizophrenia
(E) Schizophrenia, depression

447. All of the following are symptoms of schizophrenia *except*:

(A) Delusions
(B) Hallucinations
(C) Disorganized speech
(D) Manic behavior
(E) Decreased emotional expression

448. Robert has been immobile for the past two years. In fact, he keeps both his arms up in the air for two-hour periods throughout the day. Robert has been diagnosed with:

(A) Somatoform disorder
(B) Paranoid schizophrenia
(C) Conversion disorder
(D) Disorganized schizophrenia
(E) Catatonic schizophrenia

449. Which of the following is an example of a positive symptom of schizophrenia?

(A) Hallucinations
(B) Dulled emotions
(C) Little inclination to speak
(D) Loss of normal functions
(E) Intellectual impairment

450. Research has shown that individuals with schizophrenia reportedly have a:

(A) Larger hypothalamus
(B) Smaller hypothalamus
(C) Larger thalamus
(D) Smaller thalamus
(E) Smaller medulla

451. Khloe walked into a police station looking disheveled and confused. She could not remember her name, didn't recall where she came from, and couldn't remember anything about her past. Khloe has experienced:

(A) Dissociative amnesia
(B) Dissociative fugue
(C) Dissociative identity disorder
(D) Schizophrenia
(E) Antisocial personality disorder

452. Researchers have determined that there is a genetic marker in the development of schizophrenia. To test this theory, researchers used which of the following groups?

(A) Fraternal twins
(B) Siblings
(C) Parents and children
(D) Unrelated individuals
(E) Identical twins

453. Research suggests there is a direct correlation between the presence of major depression and:

(A) Moderate levels of dopamine
(B) Decreased levels of serotonin
(C) Increased levels of endorphins
(D) Enlarged hypothalamus
(E) Enlarged parietal lobe

454. Autism is considered to be a:

(A) Developmental disorder
(B) Mood disorder
(C) Learning disability
(D) Personality disorder
(E) Dissociative disorder

455. Narcissistic personality disorder is characterized by:

(A) An unstable self-image
(B) Feelings of inadequacy
(C) Social isolation
(D) Inflated sense of self
(E) Compulsive tendencies

CHAPTER 24

Therapies

456. The analysis of a client's past experiences and suggestions for ways the client can overcome his or her problems that stem from these experiences is the basis for which type of therapy?

(A) Cognitive therapy
(B) Behavioral therapy
(C) Psychoanalytic therapy
(D) Developmental therapy
(E) Social-cognitive therapy

457. Which of the following examples best illustrates insight therapy?

(A) A client takes various psychoactive drugs to treat a mental disorder.
(B) A therapist and client work together with the goal of identifying the problem and reaching a possible solution.
(C) The therapist and client discuss key traumatic issues faced by the client in his or her childhood.
(D) This therapy involves combining various techniques from many different therapeutic approaches.
(E) The therapist focuses on the thoughts of the unconscious and brings these thoughts to the surface through dream analysis.

458. Which of the following is one major difference between a clinical psychologist and a psychiatrist?

(A) A psychiatrist uses biomedical treatment.
(B) A psychiatrist uses an eclectic approach.
(C) A psychiatrist cannot counsel clients.
(D) A psychiatrist recognizes the importance of group therapy.
(E) A psychiatrist treats clients in hospitals.

459. Which of the following disorders has, in some circumstances, been treated with electroconvulsive therapy?

(A) Paranoid personality disorder
(B) Obsessive-compulsive disorder
(C) Schizophrenia
(D) Major depression
(E) Dissociative identity disorder

460. Joy's therapist is trying to encourage her to take charge of the therapy session. The therapist uses active listening while Joy discusses her feelings. Which therapy is most likely being described?

(A) Psychodynamic therapy
(B) Rational emotive therapy
(C) Existential therapy
(D) Cognitive-behavioral therapy
(E) Client-centered therapy

461. The antidepressant drug Prozac does which of the following?

(A) Blocks the reuptake of serotonin
(B) Blocks the reuptake of dopamine
(C) Levels the amount of epinephrine
(D) Deceases the amount of adrenaline in the blood stream
(E) Decreases the level of acetylcholine in the blood stream

462. Albert Ellis devised a therapy that can be very confrontational. The client must face the irrationality of his or her belief system. What is the name of this form of therapy?

(A) Cognitive-behavioral therapy
(B) Gestalt therapy
(C) Rational emotive therapy
(D) Insight therapy
(E) Social-cognitive therapy

463. Aversive therapy refers to:

(A) An operant conditioning therapy that uses negative reinforcement to continued behavior
(B) A classically conditioned therapy based on the theory that repeated pairings of negative effects lead to extinction
(C) Using generalization to let all negative behavior pairings occur
(D) Spontaneous recovery occurring long after a behavior that was based on negative pairing has ended
(E) The use of modeling behavior so clients can see the consequences of negative behaviors

464. Gestalt therapy includes which of the following?

(A) Free association
(B) Electro-shock therapy
(C) Behavioral therapy
(D) Dream analysis
(E) Biomedical therapy

465. The process by which a client expresses strong emotion toward the therapist is known as which of the following?

(A) Transference
(B) Free association
(C) Dynamic therapy
(D) Resistance
(E) Projection

466. Which of the following is a major goal of Aaron Beck's cognitive therapy?

(A) To rid an individual of his or her internal negative thought process
(B) To change an individual's negative behavior
(C) To enable a person to become self-actualized
(D) To stop individuals from using selective attention
(E) To help a client change learned or modeled behavior

467. Jana wants to be a doctor when she grows up, but she has one serious problem; she is terribly afraid of blood. Since she was a little girl she has passed out at the mere sight of blood. To overcome this fear so that she can pursue her dream of becoming a doctor, her therapist exposes her to blood while trying to relax her. What type of therapy is this?

(A) Social-cognitive therapy
(B) Systematic desensitization
(C) Behavioral therapy
(D) Rational emotive therapy
(E) Extinction

468. One major difference between a humanist therapist and a behavioral therapist is that:

(A) A behavioral therapist focuses on one's childhood.
(B) A humanist therapist pays attention to uncovering unconscious conflict.
(C) A behavioral therapist can offer medication to her or his clients.
(D) A humanist therapist focuses more on empathy and support for her or his clients.
(E) A behavioral therapist places all of the burden on the client for her or his own healing.

469. Rational emotive therapy was designed to:

(A) Teach clients relaxation techniques
(B) Explore the unconscious conflicts from a client's childhood
(C) Challenge the self-defeating thoughts of the client
(D) Use antidepressant medication to overcome depression
(E) Use free association to uncover unconscious thoughts and feelings

470. The purpose of free association is to:

(A) Help bring unconscious conflict to the surface
(B) Facilitate changing negative behaviors
(C) Change the client's thought process
(D) Rid an individual of his or her sexual desires
(E) Help a patient relax

471. Light therapy is used to help which of the following disorders?

(A) Major depression
(B) Dysthymic disorder
(C) Obsessive-compulsive disorder
(D) Dissociative identity disorder
(E) Seasonal affective disorder

472. Which of the following terms is *not* associated with psychoanalysis?

(A) Self-actualization
(B) Free association
(C) Dream analysis
(D) Hypnosis
(E) Sexual impulse

473. Which of the following psychologists believed that some people tend to have a pessimistic explanatory style, characterized by the tendency to blame bad events on themselves?

(A) Aaron Beck
(B) Martin Seligman
(C) Karen Horney
(D) Sigmund Freud
(E) Abraham Maslow

474. What is the name of the widely used therapy that involves giving an individual immediate information about the degree to which he or she can change anxiety-related responses, thereby improving control over his or her physiological process of arousal?

(A) Behavior modification
(B) Systematic desensitization
(C) Behavioral therapy
(D) Biofeedback
(E) Cognitive therapy

475. Which of the following therapies has been found affective in treating anxiety disorders, drug addictions, and autism?

(A) Psychoanalysis
(B) Social-cognitive therapy
(C) Behavioral therapy
(D) Biomedical feedback
(E) Gestalt therapy

CHAPTER 25

Social Psychology

476. John F. Kennedy's Bay of Pigs failure was caused in large part by:

(A) Brainstorming
(B) Group cohesion
(C) Groupthink
(D) Deindividuation
(E) Diffusion of responsibility

477. Solomon Asch is most famous for his research on:

(A) Conformity
(B) Obedience
(C) Compliance
(D) Cohesion
(E) Polarization

478. When we perform well on a task we typically attribute our success to our internal characteristics. This is known as:

(A) Fundamental attribution error
(B) Self-serving bias
(C) Self schema
(D) External attribution error
(E) Person schema

479. The Stanford Prison experiment was a prime example of which of the following concepts?

(A) Conformity
(B) Compliance
(C) Obedience
(D) Cohesiveness
(E) Identification

480. According to the theory of cognitive dissonance, attitudes are changed because:

(A) We are rewarded by society when our beliefs coincide with the majority.
(B) Logical arguments compel us to alter our attitudes.
(C) Emotionally persuasive arguments motivate us to change our thought process.
(D) A state of tension motivates us to change our cognitive inconsistencies by making our beliefs more consistent.
(E) When our beliefs and behaviors are too similar it causes an unpleasant psychological state of tension.

481. A person who agrees to a small request initially is more likely to comply with a larger demand later. This describes which phenomenon?

(A) Door-in-face effect
(B) Foot-in-door effect
(C) Low-ball technique
(D) High-ball technique
(E) Door-in-foot technique

482. In Milgram's experiment, subjects who gave large shocks rationalized that they were *not* personally responsible for their actions. This raises questions about our willingness to commit inhumane acts as a result of:

(A) Coercive power
(B) Expert influence
(C) Obedience to authority
(D) Conformity to group pressure
(E) Individual compliance

483. Which of the following was a factor in determining the degree of obedience in Milgram's series of experiments?

(A) Distance between the teacher and the learner
(B) Tone of voice of the teacher
(C) Whether or not the teacher was male or female
(D) Whether or not the teacher was an expert in his or her field
(E) The age of the teacher

484. In a situation in which an individual is having a seizure on the street, helping could be inhibited by which of the following concepts?

(A) Groupthink
(B) Social comparison theory
(C) Risky shift
(D) Diffusion of responsibility
(E) Compliance

485. When making the "attribution error," we tend to overestimate the importance of ________________ when judging the behaviors of others.

(A) Situational factors
(B) Personal factors
(C) Gender
(D) Intelligence
(E) Age

486. Through his experiments, Solomon Asch was able to demonstrate that:

(A) People will always conform in a group setting.
(B) Obedience to authority is determined by the perceived power of the authority figure.
(C) Size of majority does not influence how many people will conform.
(D) Compliance occurs in large groups.
(E) Lack of unanimity greatly reduces the pressure to conform.

487. One reason why many groups have some form of initiation rites and rituals is to have:

(A) Group norms
(B) Deindividuation
(C) Group cohesion
(D) Task-oriented groups
(E) Socially oriented groups

488. The Lapierre experiment proved that:

(A) People's behavior usually corresponds with their attitudes.
(B) People's attitudes do not necessarily reflect their behavior.
(C) People tend to lie when asked to fill out a survey.
(D) People are obedient in front of any person of authority.
(E) Most people conform because of fear of embarrassment.

489. Damion rewrote his paper at the suggestion of his professor, even though he did not agree with the suggestions. This is an example of:

(A) Obedience
(B) Conformity
(C) Compliance
(D) Diffusion
(E) Cognitive dissonance

490. Which of the following scenarios is an example of deindividuation?

(A) Cindy finds that working in her group brings high levels of performance compared to students who work alone.
(B) Mindy forms a study group because she wants academic help, social support, and motivation.
(C) Amy has a poor running performance in competition; she performs even worse in front of a larger crowd.
(D) Torrie honks her horn loudly for quite a while because she has little chance of being personally identified.
(E) Jamie does not help the girl being attacked because the other bystanders are taking little action.

491. When group discussions change individuals' judgments, it is known as:

(A) Risky shift
(B) Groupthink
(C) Group polarization
(D) Social comparison
(E) Group cohesion

492. Which of the following examples best illustrates a way to avoid groupthink from occurring?

(A) Choose a group captain to make all the final decisions.
(B) Allow the group's members the freedom to express differing opinions.
(C) Have every group member come in with a specific idea to bring to the table.
(D) Only allow one person in the group to speak at a time.
(E) Make the group socially oriented before making any final decisions.

493. Of the following examples, which would be the best example of self-serving bias?

(A) Michael, who believes that everyone should give to charities
(B) Paris, who believes she failed her math test even though she always gets an A in math
(C) Janet, who is always her teacher's favorite student
(D) Randy, who believes he works harder than others and is underappreciated
(E) Rebi, who overestimates her ability to run the after-school program for young children

494. After Jean was told by one of her professors that she would never succeed in law school, she stopped reading and completing her assignments. Eventually Jean did drop out of law school. This is an example of:

(A) Self-fulfilling prophecy
(B) Self-serving bias
(C) Social loafing
(D) Groupthink
(E) Diffusion of responsibility

495. David has always opposed the death penalty, believing it is not the place of the government to take the life of another person. After his best friend was murdered, David wanted nothing more than to see the murderer get the justice he or she deserved. Because the murder occurred in the state of Texas, this would mean justice would be served with the death penalty. The dissonance theory would state that:

(A) David would have no conflict in seeing the murderer put to death.
(B) David would have to change one of his attitudes to feel less tension.
(C) Justification of the death penalty would be appropriate in this situation.
(D) Morally, David would not support the death penalty under any circumstance.
(E) David would change his opinion in support of the death penalty.

496. The tendency to attribute our own behavior to situational causes and the behavior of others to personal causes is an example of:

(A) Self-fulfilling prophecy
(B) Actor-observer bias
(C) Dispositional attribution
(D) Attribution theory
(E) Just-world phenomenon

497. Evidence suggests that individuals tend to be attracted to others who are:
(A) Nearly opposite in all areas
(B) Similar to themselves in terms of perspective and values
(C) Physically more attractive than they are
(D) Unlikely to criticize or judge them
(E) Less intelligent than themselves

498. The tendency to "blame the victim" in a rape case is an example of which of the following terms?
(A) Fundamental attribution error
(B) Deindividuation
(C) Self-serving bias
(D) The just-world phenomenon
(E) Self-fulfilling prophecy

499. In the presence of the largest crowd she has ever seen, Heather gives her finest piano performance. This is an example of:
(A) Group cohesion
(B) Deindividuation
(C) Group polarization
(D) Social inhibition
(E) Social facilitation

500. According to the diffusion of responsibility theory, the biggest factor in predicting whether or not a bystander will help someone in need is:
(A) The duration of the situation
(B) Whether or not the person in need of help is male or female
(C) The number of other bystanders at the scene
(D) The level of perceived threat
(E) Whether or not the person actually asked for help

ANSWERS

Chapter 1: Schools of Thought

1. (A) Cognitive psychology is the study of how we process, store, and retrieve information. Choices (B) and (C) are devoted to studying the way people relate to others and the unique attributes of a person; neither field focuses on one's thought process. (D) deals with long-lasting changes in behavior, usually through experience. (E) is the experience of a meaningful pattern of a stimulus.

2. (C) Abraham Maslow is a humanist. The humanist approach emphasizes that each individual has free will to determine his or her own future. Self-actualization is an inherent tendency to reach our true potential.

3. (D) Wertheimer, along with Wolfgang Kohler and Kurt Koffka, studied the illusion of flashing lights and the perception of movement. Wertheimer argued that perceptual experiences, such as flashing lights, resulted from a "whole pattern" or, in German, "Gestalt."

4. (A) William James wrote the *Principles of Psychology*, published in 1890. This book included the study of the mind, sensation, memory, and reasoning. James is associated with functionalism. Wundt is associated with structuralism. Watson is associated with behaviorism. Freud is associated with psychoanalysis. Wertheimer is associated with Gestalt.

5. (A) John Watson published a paper called "Psychology as a Behaviorist Views It." Watson rejected the notion that introspection can be used as a technique to determine the behavior of human beings. Watson believed psychology needed to be an objective experimental science. Unlike choices (B), (C), (D), and (E), behaviorism was the first field to study psychology in an observable and measurable manner.

6. (D) The definition of the eclectic approach is a combination of techniques and ideas from many different schools of thought in psychology.

7. (D) The psychoanalytic approach focuses on the idea that each of us has an unconscious that contains thoughts, desires, and fears that have been hidden or repressed because they threaten our conscious self. (A), rewards and punishments, is based on behaviorism. (B), self-esteem and self-actualization, is based on humanism.

8. (A) In Pavlov's experiment in which he rang a bell before putting food in the dogs' mouths, the dogs eventually paired the bell with salivating, even when the food was not present. This phenomenon, which Pavlov called conditioned reflex, eventually became known as classical conditioning. Because this theory was based on involuntary reflexes and many psychologists believe human behavior is based on voluntary choices, they criticized classical conditioning, claiming it could not help us further understand human behavior. This explanation negates choice (C). (D) and (E) are irrelevant to this question.

9. (B) Wilhelm Wundt established the first psychological laboratory in 1879. Structuralism is the study of the most basic elements in our conscious minds. John Watson was a behaviorist. William James studied functionalism. Max Wertheimer studied Gestalt. Sigmund Freud studied psychoanalysis.

10. (B) The behavioral approach analyzes how organisms learn or modify behavior based on rewards and punishments in the environment. The other choices do not specifically focus on reinforcements in one's environment.

11. (D) The behavioral approach emphasizes the objective, scientific analysis of observable behavior. This includes conditioning human behavior. Choice (A) focuses on an individual's thought process or perception. Choices (B) and (C) were both schools of thought that focused on introspection. Psychoanalysis emphasized the strength of the unconscious.

12. (B) Wilhelm Wundt is considered the father of psychology. Wundt established the first psychological laboratory in 1879.

13. (C) Structuralism was influenced by the physical scientists of the time. Wundt emphasized that all complex substances could be separated into component elements, whereas functionalists examined behaviors from a different point of view. Functionalists were asking what the mind does and why. Choice (C) best exemplifies these concepts. (A) is too vague and inaccurate to be the correct answer. (B) does not represent either structuralism or functionalism. (D) is incorrect because both structuralism and functionalism used introspection as a means of determining human behavior. Once again, choice (E) is not using accurate information to define either structuralism or functionalism.

14. (E) The basis of humanism is the understanding that individuals have free will and a large capacity for reaching their potential. It is the human experience that we all share that enables individuals to attain such goals. Cognitive psychology is incorrect because it focuses on the process of thinking, perception, and attention to details of language and problem solving. Cognition does not emphasize the human experience. Structuralism focuses on complex mental elements. Behaviorism is based on relationships, stimulus-response, and rewards and punishments. Functionalists examined mental processes, not human experience.

15. (A) Psychoanalysis stresses the importance of the patient and psychologist working together to explore the client's past. Humanism emphasizes one's present and future, not one's past. Cognitive psychology works on changing the client's way of thinking, again not placing much emphasis on the past. Eclectic simply means using several different approaches of psychology. Behavioral psychology tries to identify negative behaviors and eliminate them through such means as systematic desensitization.

16. (D) Psychodynamic psychology stresses the influence of the unconscious. Its fears, impulses, and desires motivate our conscious behavior. Choice (A), free will and self-actualization, refers to humanism. (B) refers to experimental psychology. (C) refers to part of Carl Jung's theory of personality development.

17. (B) Developmental psychologists study a person's biological, emotional, cognitive, and social development across the life span. Choice (A) is too vague to be the correct answer. (C) is incorrect because mental process refers to cognitive psychology, not developmental psychology. (D) and (E) are incorrect because they do not answer the question.

18. (A) Choice (A) is the definition of phenomenology, the study of natural, unanalyzed perception.

19. (C) Biological psychologists focus on the ways changes in an organism's physical makeup can affect behavior, relating directly to genetics and the nervous system. Choices (A), (B), and (D) are incorrect because biological psychologists do not study the mind or life experiences. Choice (E) may appear to be correct, but the question is asking what the term *biological psychology* refers to, which is not drug treatment.

20. (A) Choice (A) is the definition for a case study. Choice (B) defines a longitudinal study. Choice (E) defines a cross-sectional study. Choices (C) and (D) do not define any type of study.

Chapter 2: Research Methods

21. (D) A correlation expresses a relationship between two variables without ascribing cause. Correlational research employs statistical methods to examine a relationship between two or more variables, but does not permit researchers to draw conclusions. Unlike correlational research, experimental research offers the opportunity to draw conclusions because of the strict control of variables.

22. (A) A random sample is defined as a sample in which each potential participant has an equal chance of selection. Choice (B) defines *representative sample.* Choice (C) defines the term *sample,* not *random sample.* Choices (D) and (E) do not accurately define *random sample.*

23. (C) While researchers were testing the hypothesis that better lighting would boost worker output in an electric plant in the 1920s, they were surprised to see their results showed something else entirely. Productivity increased regardless of lighting merely because of the researcher's attention and not factory conditions. Choice (A) is incorrect because the Hawthorne effect focuses on the researcher's attention, not expectations. Choice (B) refers to the researcher's bias and change of behavior, not the subject's.

24. (E) A confounding variable is anything that differs between the control group and the experimental group besides the independent variable. How fast and hungry the mice are at the beginning of the experiment are potential confounding variables. When and where the race takes place are also possible confounding variables that can potentially change the findings of this experiment. The population from which the mice were selected cannot be a confounding variable. This will not differ for the two groups. All of the mice were chosen from the same larger population. Even if this larger population is flawed, it is not considered a confounding variable.

25. (B) Marc has established a relationship. Marc did not conduct an experiment; therefore, he cannot draw any conclusions. Marc has found a correlation between studying and performance on a final exam; whether or not it is significant would require the use of inferential statistics.

26. (E) Jordan would need to use inferential statistics to determine whether the experimental group's aggression levels were significantly different. Jordan could very well use descriptive statistics, but not before he determines whether his hypothesis has been supported and represents the larger population.

27. (C) Correlational research allows the researcher to determine whether a relationship exists between two variables. A positive correlation means that high scores on one variable tend to be paired with high scores on the other variable. A number between −1 and +1 expresses the strength of the correlation. A negative correlation means that high scores on one variable tend to be paired with low scores on the other variable. The number 0 denotes the weakest possible correlation or no correlation at all.

28. (A) A negative correlation is expressed as −1. This means that as one variable goes up, the other variable will go down. In this case, as the room temperature went up, the student performance went down, indicating a negative correlation.

29. (B) The independent variable in the experiment is the variable that is manipulated to test its effects on the other, dependent variables. In this experiment, the manipulation of the number of alcoholic drinks given to the subjects will affect their levels of aggression. The dependent variable in the experiment is measured to see how it is changed from the manipulation of the independent variable.

30. (C) With experimental research the strict control of variables offers the researcher the opportunity to draw conclusions about cause-and-effect relationships. In this instance, if the researcher wants to establish a causal relationship between eating breakfast and work performance, experimental research must be used. Correlational research does not allow the researcher to draw conclusions. Surveys simply allow the researcher to gather an immense amount of data in a short period of time.

Chapter 3: The Brain

31. (A) The Broca's area is located in the left frontal lobe. It is necessary for combining sounds into words and arranging words into meaningful sentences. Wernicke's area plays a role in understanding speech. The hypothalamus is part of the limbic system and regulates motivational and emotional behavior. The hippocampus is involved in transferring fleeting memories into permanent storage. The medulla is responsible for heart rate and blood pressure.

32. (C) The cerebellum is a region of the hindbrain that is involved in motor control and coordinating movements. Damage to this region would therefore cause loss of muscular coordination.

33. (C) The pons is a bridge that connects the spinal cord to the brain. Cells in the pons manufacture chemicals involved in sleep.

34. (E) The reticular formation arouses and alerts the forebrain and prepares it to receive information from all other senses. Damage to this location can cause permanent unconsciousness. Damage to the temporal lobe can cause speech and language issues. Damage to the frontal lobe can cause motivational and emotional issues. Damage to the parietal lobe can cause sensory motor issues.

35. (C) By measuring electrical impulses, an EEG (electro-encephalogram) can detect epileptic seizures, covert processing, seizure disorders, and sleep disorders.

36. (B) The corpus callosum is a wide band of fibers that connect the left and the right hemispheres of the brain. It has 200 million neural fibers that allow information to pass back and forth between the hemispheres. It was believed that by cutting the corpus callosum, in what was known as a "split-brain" operation, people suffering from epilepsy could decrease the number of seizures they had.

37. (A) The limbic system is a group of about half a dozen interconnected structures in the core of the forebrain that are involved in many motivational behaviors, such as eating, drinking, and sexual desire. Breathing regulations are controlled by the medulla. The cerebellum controls balance and coordination. Various regions in the left hemisphere of the brain control speech and language.

38. (A) The thalamus is often referred to as the "switchboard" of the brain. All sensory information that enters the brain goes through the thalamus. It is the job of the thalamus to relay the information to the appropriate region of the brain.

39. (D) The parietal lobe is located directly behind the frontal lobe. Its functions include processing sensory information from the body parts, which includes touching, locating limb positions, and feeling temperature. The occipital lobe is responsible for processing visual information. The temporal lobe is responsible for processing auditory information. The frontal lobe is responsible for interpreting and performing emotional behavior, behaving normally in social situations, and maintaining a healthy personality.

40. (B) Damage to the Broca's area will result in Broca's aphasia, which means a person cannot speak in fluent sentences but can understand written and spoken words.

41. (B) The occipital lobe is critical for recognizing objects. Damage to this area results in difficulties of recognition, a condition called visual agnosia. In visual agnosia the individual fails to recognize some object, person, or color, yet has the ability to see and describe parts of some visual stimuli.

42. (B) The patient will be able to say she saw the word ART because it was projected to the left hemisphere, which has the ability to control speech. Although the patient's right hemisphere saw the word HE, the right hemisphere turns out to be mute, meaning that it cannot say what it saw. However, the patient can point with her left hand to a photo of HE, indicating the right hemisphere understood the question.

43. (E) The somatosensory cortex is a narrow strip of the cortex that is located at the front edge of the parietal lobe. It processes sensory information about touch, location of limbs, pain, and temperature.

44. (C) The amygdala is involved in forming, recognizing, and remembering emotional experiences, unlike the hippocampus, which is responsible for transferring fleeting memories into permanent storage.

45. (A) An MRI, or magnetic resonance imaging, involves passing nonharmful radio frequencies through the brain. A PET scan, or positron emission tomography, involves injecting slightly radioactive solutions into the bloodstream.

46. (B) The midbrain is involved in visual and auditory reflexes, such as automatically turning your head toward a noise. The hindbrain has three distinct structures: the pons, the medulla, and the cerebellum. The forebrain is responsible for a large number of functions, including learning and memory. The motor cortex is involved in the initiation of all voluntary movements.

47. (E) Choice (E) is the only career that needs some amount of creativity, which is controlled by the right hemisphere. The other choices are all careers that need strong language, logical reasoning, and writing skills. The left hemisphere controls these skills. Damage to the left hemisphere would make those careers difficult.

48. (C) Balance and coordination are controlled by the cerebellum. All of the other choices are controlled by the hypothalamus.

49. (C) The limbic system is a group of structures in the forebrain that are involved in motivational behavior. The four structures that make up the limbic system are the hippocampus, hypothalamus, thalamus, and amygdala.

50. (A) The Wernicke's area is located in the left temporal lobe. This area plays a role in understanding speech.

Chapter 4: Neuroscience

51. (D) The myelin sheath is composed of fatty material that wraps around and insulates an axon. The axon is a single threadlike structure that carries signals away from the cell body. The dendrites are branchlike extensions that arise from the cell body. The synapse is a small space that exists between an end bulb and adjacent cell body. The cell body provides fuel and maintains the neuron.

52. (C) Another name for the cell body is the soma, a relatively large structure that maintains the entire neuron.

53. (A) If a stimulus is large enough to excite a neuron, two things will happen to the axon. First the stimulus will eventually open the axon's chemical gates by stopping the sodium pump. Second, when the stoppage of the sodium pump causes the gate to open, thousands of positive ions will rush in. The action potential is a tiny electrical current that is generated when positive sodium ions rush into the axon. A resting state is when the axon has a charge, like a battery, with positive ions on the outside and negative ions on the inside.

54. (A) When you step on a sharp object, you seem to feel the pain almost immediately. Neurons send signals at speeds as high as 200 miles per hour. To feel the pain involves several events happening in this order: The stimulus—in this example, stepping on a nail—begins the reaction. Sensors in your skin then pick up the mechanical pressure and transforms it into an electrical impulse. When the impulse reaches the end bulb it releases the neurotransmitter, which is the chemical messenger that transmits information between nerves and body organs. Since the stimulus must come first, choices (B), (C), and (D) can be eliminated. Choice (E) is incorrect because the neurotransmitter has to be released before anything can reach the receptor site.

55. (B) The sodium pump is a transport process that picks up any sodium ions that enter the axon's chemical gates and returns them back outside. Choice (A) is incorrect because when the axon is charged, positive ions are on the outside while negative ions are on the inside. Choices (C) and (D) do not correctly define a sodium pump. Choice (E) is incorrect because the sodium pump is not a neural impulse.

56. (D) The all-or-none law is the principle that the action potential in a neuron does not vary in strength; the neuron either fires at full strength or it does not fire at all. Choice (B) is incorrect because the synapse is the area composed of the axon terminal of one neuron and the dendrite of the next neuron. Choice (C) is incorrect because the resting state is when a neuron is positively charged outside and negatively charged on the inside. Choice (E) is incorrect because the sodium pump is a transport process that picks up sodium ions.

57. (C) Threatening or challenging physical or psychological stimuli triggers the sympathetic nervous system. This increases physiological arousal and prepares the body for action. The sympathetic nervous system prepares the body for "fight or flight." The parasympathetic nervous system helps return the body to equilibrium, also called homeostasis.

58. (B) Alcohol affects the nervous system in a number of ways, blocking neural receptors and stimulating others. Some neurons are excited by the neurotransmitter GABA, which the brain normally manufactures. Alcohol molecules so closely resemble those of GABA neurotransmitters that alcohol can function like GABA and open GABA receptors. Anandamide is involved in memory, motor coordination, and emotions. Dopamine is critical to the way the brain controls movement; there is a direct link to dopamine levels in the body and Parkinson's disease and schizophrenia. Acetylcholine is a major excitatory neurotransmitter. Serotonin influences mood levels in the body.

59. (A) The sympathetic nervous system and parasympathetic nervous system are both subdivisions of the autonomic nervous system. The sympathetic nervous system prepares the body for threatening or challenging situations, which means increased blood pressure and increased heart rate. The parasympathetic nervous system returns the body to a relaxed state, for example, decreased heart rate.

60. (E) Efferent neurons carry information away from the spinal cord to produce responses in various muscles. Afferent neurons carry information from the senses to the spinal cord. Interneurons carry information within the central nervous system.

Chapter 5: Sensation and Perception

61. (A) Sensation is the experience of sensory stimulation. Perception is the process of creating meaningful patterns from the sensory information. Adaptation is the decreasing response of the sense organs upon exposure to a continual stimulation.

62. (C) The minimum intensity of physical energy required to produce any sensation at all in a person is called absolute threshold. The difference threshold, also known as the just-noticeable difference, is the smallest change in stimulation that can be detected 50 percent of the time.

63. (B) Weber's law states that the JND (just-noticeable difference) for any given sense is a proportion of the stimulation being judged. Hearing, for example, is very sensitive: we can detect a 0.3 percent change in sound. By contrast, producing a JND in taste requires a 20 percent change.

64. (E) The transparent protective coating over the front part of the eye is the cornea. The lens focuses the light onto the retina. The iris is the colored part of the eye. The pupil is the small opening in the iris where light enters. The fovea is the area of the retina that is the center of the visual field.

65. (B) The lens is the transparent part of the eye inside the pupil that focuses light onto the retina.

66. (D) The photoreceptors with a conelike shape are called cones. They are primarily located in the center of the retina, called the fovea. The fovea is the correct answer, and not the retina, because the question was looking for the location of the greatest density of cones.

67. (A) An afterimage is a visual sensation that continues after the original stimulus is removed. For example, if you stare at a blue square, you will see a yellow afterimage.

68. (C) On the basis of his work with afterimages, physiologist Ewald Hering suggested that the visual system codes colors by using two complementary pairs: red/green and blue/yellow. Hering's idea became known as the opponent-process theory. The trichromatic theory says there are three different kinds of cones in the retina, not related to an afterimage. The volley principle has to do with receptors in the ear and has no relation to an afterimage.

69. (B) Trichromats are people who have normal color vision. Trichromats perceive all hues by combining the colors red, blue, and green.

70. (D) The three small bones are called the hammer, anvil, and stirrup, also known as the ossicles.

71. (B) Transduction refers to the process in which a sense organ, in this case the nose, changes or transforms physical energy into electrical signals that become neural impulses, which may be sent to the brain for processing. Choice (A) is incorrect because adaptation refers to a decreased response to a stimulation. Choice (C) is incorrect because sensation is a meaningless bit of information. Choice (D) is incorrect because perception is meaningful sensory experiences.

72. (C) A gymnast relies on both her kinesthetic and her vestibular senses. Her kinesthetic senses are relaying messages pertaining to muscle strain and movements; her vestibular senses are supplying feedback about her body position. Kinesthetic senses are senses of muscle movement, posture, and strain on muscles and joints. Vestibular senses are the senses of equilibrium and body position.

73. (B) Loudness is our subjective experience of a sound's intensity. The brain calculates loudness from specific physical energy, in this case the amplitude of sound waves. Pitch is our subjective experience of a sound being high or low. The frequency of the sound wave is measured in cycles.

74. (D) The olfactory cells are located in two one-inch-square patches of tissue in the uppermost part of the nasal passages.

75. (A) Convergence is a binocular cue for depth perception based on signals sent from muscles that turn the eye. To focus on near or approaching objects, these muscles turn the eyes inward, toward the nose. Retinal disparity refers to the different position of the eyes receiving slightly different images. Shape constancy refers to the tendency to perceive an object as retaining the same shape even when you view it from different angles. Interposition comes into play when objects overlap.

76. (C) Size constancy refers to our tendency to perceive objects as remaining the same size even when their images on the retina are continually growing or shrinking. Choice (A), shape constancy, refers to changing shapes, not necessarily size.

77. (E) Convergence is a binocular cue, meaning the cue depends on the movement of both eyes. Choices (A), (B), (C), and (D) are monocular cues, that is, cues that are produced from a single eye.

78. (C) The cochlea is located in the inner ear. The cochlea contains the receptors for hearing, and its function is transduction, transforming vibrations into nerve impulses that are sent to the brain for processing into auditory information.

79. (B) The gate control theory explains that you may not notice pain from a headache or injury while thoroughly involved in some other activity, because impulses from that activity close the neural gate and block the passage of painful impulses.

80. (D) Rods are photoreceptors that contain a single chemical, called rhodopsin, which is activated by small amounts of light. Because rods are extremely light sensitive, they allow us to see in dim light, but to see only black, white, and shades of gray. Cones are photoreceptors that contain three chemicals called opsins, which are activated in bright light and allow us to see color.

Chapter 6: Consciousness, Sleep, and Dreams

81. (D) Altered states of consciousness result from using any number of procedures, such as meditation, psychoactive drugs, hypnosis, or sleep deprivation. Choices (A), (B), (C), and (E) all differ from normal consciousness. The chief characteristic of these altered states, unlike exercise, is that we perceive our internal and external environments in ways different from normal perception.

82. (A) The automatic process is any activity that requires little awareness, takes minimal attention, and does not interfere with ongoing activities. All of these characteristics describe what sometimes happens while people are driving a familiar route. Choice (B) requires full awareness. Choices (C), (D), and (E) do not pertain to this question.

83. (B) The circadian rhythm refers to a biological clock that is genetically programmed to regulate physiological responses within a time period of 24–25 hours (one day). Most of us operate on a 24-hour day and thus set back our sleep-wake circadian clock about one hour each day. Choice (A), interval timing clock, works more like a stopwatch, which helps a person to time his or her movements, such as knowing when to start or stop an activity. Choice (C), biological clock, is an internal timing device used to regulate various physiological responses, but it is not genetically programmed.

84. (D) Melatonin is a hormone that is secreted by the pineal gland. Melatonin secretion increases with darkness and decreases with light, playing a role in the regulation of circadian rhythms and in promoting sleep. Serotonin is related to mood levels and mood control. Norepinephrine works as a stress hormone and is directly related to "fight or flight." Epinephrine, when produced by the body, increases heart rate and blood pressure. Dopamine also relates to the sympathetic nervous system, increasing heart rate and blood pressure.

85. (B) Stage 1 sleep is a transition stage from wakefulness to sleep. In this stage a person gradually loses responsiveness to stimuli and experiences drifting thoughts and images. REM sleep, or paradoxical sleep, is marked by physiological arousal and voluntary muscle paralysis. Stage 2 sleep marks the beginning of a deeper sleep. Stages 3 and 4 are characterized by low-frequency waves; stage 4 specifically is considered to be the deepest sleep stage.

86. (A) Stage 4 sleep is also called slow wave, or delta, sleep. It is characterized by waves of very high amplitude and low frequency, called delta waves.

87. (D) REM sleep is also known as paradoxical sleep. REM brain waves have fast frequency and low amplitude and look very similar to beta waves, which occur when you are wide-awake. During this stage your body is physiologically aroused, but your voluntary muscles are paralyzed. REM sleep stage is highly associated with dreaming.

88. (D) Sleepwalking and sleep talking do occur during stage 4 sleep. Many people confuse this answer with REM stage, because of the belief that sleepwalkers and sleep talkers are acting out their dreams that occur in REM. But voluntary muscles are paralyzed during REM; therefore, people cannot physically act out their dreams. Because stage 4 is the deepest stage of sleep, very often people do not remember sleepwalking or sleep talking.

89. (C) From infancy to adolescence, the total amount of time spent in sleep and the percentage spent in REM gradually decline. Newborns sleep about 17 hours a day, and 50 percent of that time is spent in REM. A four-year-old sleeps about 10 hours, and 25 percent of that time is spent in REM. From adolescence to old age, we maintain the same amount of sleep time, approximately 7.5 hours of sleep, and the same percentage of REM sleep, about 20 percent or less.

90. (B) Choice (B) defines the term *adaptive sleep theory*. Support for the adaptive theory comes from observations that large predatory animals sleep more and wherever they want, while smaller prey sleep less and in more protected areas. Choice (A) defines the term *repair theory*.

91. (C) The activation-synthesis theory of dreams says that dreaming represents the random and meaningless activity of nerve cells in the brain. Choices (A) and (B) represent the Freudian view of dreaming. Choice (E) represents the extension of waking life theory.

92. (A) REM sleep, which stands for "rapid eye movement," is associated with dreaming. Dream research suggests that about 80–90 percent of the times when subjects are awakened from REM sleep, they report having had a vivid and long dream. Only about 5–10 percent of our dreams occur in stage 4 sleep and are less likely to be remembered.

93. (E) Freud's view on dreaming was the belief that dreams protect the conscious from the realization of our unconscious desires and wishes, especially sexual or aggressive wishes. Our dreams transform these desires into harmless symbols and do not disturb our sleep. Extension of waking life is based on the belief that our dreams reflect the same thoughts and concerns we have when we are awake. The activation-synthesis theory suggests that dreams are a product of neural firings in our brain. The spiritual world theory states that dreams represent the time when one enters the spiritual world, which helps a person to reflect on the past, present, or future, through communication with the souls of people who are no longer with us.

94. (B) A person with sleep apnea may repeatedly stop breathing, momentarily wake up, resume breathing, and return to sleep. Narcolepsy is marked by excessive sleepiness usually in the form of sleep attacks. Insomnia refers to difficulties in either going to sleep or staying asleep through the night.

95. (A) Night terrors are frightening experiences that often start with screaming, followed by sudden waking in a fearful state with rapid breathing. They usually occur in stage 4 sleep. Night terrors are often confused with nightmares, which usually occur during REM sleep. They are also frightening, but usually produce clear anxiety-producing images.

96. (C) Narcolepsy is a chronic disorder. It is characterized by sleep attacks or short lapses of sleep throughout the day. These attacks are accompanied by REM sleep and muscle paralysis.

97. (B) REM sleep looks very similar to beta waves. Physiologically a person is aroused during this stage and muscles are paralyzed, which is why this stage is known as "paradoxical sleep." Choice (A) is incorrect because REM sleep is not the deepest stage of sleep; stage 4 is. Choice (C) is incorrect because body paralysis occurs during REM; therefore, a person cannot sleepwalk. Choice (D) is incorrect because night terrors occur in stage 4 sleep, not REM. Choice (E) is incorrect because a person's vital signs are actually very aroused in REM.

98. (E) Waking consciousness is a mental state that encompasses all thoughts and perceptions that occur when we are awake. The altered state of consciousness awareness is different from the consciously awake person. Choices (B) and (C) represent states of mind different from the consciously awake person as well.

99. (A) One of the main reasons people daydream is to escape reality. It is usually done without effort or recognition. In choices (C), (D), and (E), a person does recognize he or she is doing something to escape, usually with more effort. Dreaming, on the other hand, occurs without any recognition.

100. (C) Insomnia is difficulty with either falling asleep or staying asleep. Narcolepsy is a disorder characterized by sleep attacks. Sleep apnea is marked by periods of sleep when a person stops breathing.

101. (E) Delta waves are slow waves with a very high amplitude and very low frequency. Delta waves are part of stage 4 sleep, not REM. All of the other choices are definite characteristics of REM sleep.

102. (C) An adult getting approximately seven to eight hours of sleep will go through four to five cycles of sleep. A full cycle begins with stage 1 sleep and ends with REM. The next cycle starts at stage 2 and goes up to stage 3 and 4 and back to REM again. Individuals do not return to stage 1 until around the time they are going to wake up.

103. (B) Each stage is 90 minutes. The first cycle includes stages 1, 2, 3, 4, and REM. The next cycle begins with stage 2.

104. (A) Many psychologists in the 1950s believed that if people were denied REM sleep and therefore could not dream, they would suffer mentally and emotionally. Studies today continue to show long-term detrimental behavioral problems when people do not get enough REM sleep. This is not the case with the other stages of sleep.

105. (C) Alpha waves are characteristic of this period before entering sleep. Delta waves are characteristic of stage 4 sleep. Beta waves are characteristics of REM sleep. Theta waves are characteristic of stage 1 sleep.

106. (D) The reticular formation arouses and alerts the forebrain. It is stimulated in sleeping animals. Choices (A) and (B) have to do with memory and emotion. Choice (E) has to do with breathing and heart rate.

107. (B) Extension of waking life theory suggests that dreams reflect our thoughts and concerns from our waking lives, or issues we have on our minds when we are awake. Freud's theory suggests our dreams represent our repressed desires and fantasies. Activation synthesis suggests dreams are a product of our neural firings in the brain. Spiritual world theory suggests when we dream we are in touch with those who have passed on.

108. (E) As an adult, 80 percent of our sleep is in NREM. In other words, adults spend 20 percent of their sleep in REM sleep.

109. (A) Beta waves are characteristic of REM sleep. REM sleep is where 90 percent of our dreaming occurs; therefore, beta waves are characteristic of a person who is dreaming.

110. (A) REM rebound is the idea that we go straight to REM sleep when we are sleep deprived.

Chapter 7: Drugs and Hypnosis

111. (A) Ernest Hilgard developed the hidden observer concept. The idea was that under a hypnotic trance a person's conscious is actually divided into two parts. The hypnotized part will feel little or no pain and will respond that way orally. The unhypnotized part will feel normal pain sensations but will not answer the question orally. This part can respond to the question by tapping one's fingers.

112. (D) Morphine, cocaine, and heroin are all highly physically addictive drugs, causing a person abusing these drugs to feel an overwhelming and compulsive desire to obtain and abuse the drug. Even after stopping, the person has a great tendency to relapse and begin using the drug again.

113. (C) The definition for dependency is a change in the nervous system that results in a person's needing the drug to prevent painful withdrawal symptoms. Choice (A) defines tolerance. Choice (B) defines addiction. Choice (D) defines withdrawal symptoms.

114. (B) When excited, neurons secrete neurotransmitters. After a brief period of time, the neurotransmitters are reabsorbed back into the neuron. This process is called reuptake. If reuptake did not occur, the neurotransmitter would remain in the synapse and neurons would be continually stimulated. Cocaine blocks reuptake, which leads to increased neural stimulation, causing increased physical and psychological arousal.

115. (E) Stimulants, by definition, increase activities of the central nervous system. This results in heightened alertness, arousal, and euphoria. Cocaine, caffeine, nicotine, and amphetamines are all stimulants. Heroin is an opiate, which is highly addictive and used for pain reduction.

116. (D) Tolerance occurs after a person uses a drug repeatedly over a period of time. The drug no longer produces the desired effects. Withdrawal is the painful symptoms that occur when a person is no longer taking an addictive drug. Addiction is the behavioral pattern marked by a compulsive desire for the drug.

117. (C) Cravings for heroin, unlike other drugs, become very intense very quickly. During detoxification, a person can suffer from vomiting, nausea, diarrhea, and chills. This is part of the reason why heroin is such a powerful drug. Although the other choices are also highly addictive drugs, heroin has such severe withdrawal symptoms that it is much harder to stop.

118. (A) Hallucinogens are a separate category from stimulants, eliminating choices (B) and (E). Choice (C) describes some characteristics of opiates. Hallucinogens are not depressants, thereby eliminating choice (D).

119. (A) The most important part of hypnosis is suggestibility. This eliminates choices (B), (C), and (E). Choice (D) is incorrect because hypnotists do not tell people they are going to enter a trance; instead their suggestions are much more subtle. Some examples would be a suggestion of feeling relaxed, feeling sleepy, or having a floating feeling.

120. (D) Compared to adults, young children, especially between the ages of 8 and 12, are more susceptible to hypnosis. At this particular age range, children are often taught to listen to authority figures. They also use their imaginations more often and are more likely to believe due to the fact that they are less jaded than many adults.

121. (A) LSD, unlike the other choices, is a hallucinogen. One of the symptoms listed is hallucinations, therefore eliminating the other drugs. Cocaine and methamphetamines are stimulants. Barbiturates are depressants. Heroin is an opiate.

122. (C) Barbiturates are "downers," which means they slow down or depress the central nervous system, while amphetamines are often referred to as "uppers," which means they stimulate the central nervous system.

123. (B) This question is asking, in pretty general terms, the four major effects of psychoactive drugs. Appetite, sex drive, and digestion are too specific and therefore eliminate choices (A), (C), (D), and (E). Choice (B) gives the overall impacts of any psychoactive drugs.

124. (D) Heroin is an opiate. Opiates are generally used as painkillers. They do increase feelings of euphoria and are highly addictive. The other choices are all examples of depressants. Depressants slow down the central nervous system, decreasing anxiety and increasing relaxation.

125. **(B)** Marijuana is a hallucinogen, causing psychological effects. Marijuana is believed to act sometimes as a depressant because of its physiological effects, including relaxed inhibitions and feelings of euphoria. Choices (A), (C), (D), and (E) do not cause all of the symptoms listed in the question.

126. **(E)** Hypnosis is most commonly used to ease pain, stop unhealthy habits, and help patients recall memories. Hypnosis is not used for marriage counseling.

127. **(E)** Anton Mesmer believed a force called "animal magnetism" could pass into a patient's body, curing a variety of symptoms. The term *mesmerized*, meaning "spellbound or hypnotized," comes from Anton Mesmer.

128. **(C)** The key term in this question is *susceptible*. If a person is susceptible to hypnosis it means he or she has more than likely entered into a hypnotic trance. While under a trance, a hypnotist will suggest that the person does not feel pain. Someone who does not believe in, or has not entered into a hypnotic trance, will probably not report lower levels of pain.

129. **(E)** Posthypnotic exhortation is a made-up term. Posthypnotic amnesia is not remembering what happened during hypnosis. Hidden observer is the belief that your consciousness is divided into two parts while under a trance. Suggestibility is what allows people under hypnosis to perform a certain behavior. Hypnotic analgesia is the inability to feel pain while still conscious.

130. **(E)** Heroin is an opiate. Opiates produce withdrawal symptoms, and they are very addictive. Marijuana is not an opiate. Opiates are both physiologically and psychologically addictive.

Chapter 8: Classical Conditioning

131. **(A)** The UCS, unconditioned stimulus, is a stimulus that automatically causes an organism to respond in a specific way. In this case the substance automatically makes the coyotes ill. The CS, or conditioned stimulus, is an originally neutral stimulus that is paired with an unconditioned stimulus and eventually produces the desired responses in an organism. In this case the sheep's wool was originally neutral and is now associated with the substance. The CR, or conditioned response, is the response an organism produces when only a conditioned stimulus is present. In this case the conditioned response is the aversion to the sheep, which occurred after conditioning made an association between the substance and the sheep.

132. **(C)** Generalization is the tendency for a stimulus that is similar to the original conditioned stimulus to elicit a response that is similar to the conditioned response. In this situation, the coyotes showed the same aversion response to the nearby sheep as they did to the original flock of sheep.

133. **(D)** This is a straightforward definition question. Choice (D) clearly defines the Premack Principle.

134. (A) *Variable interval* means an unspecified amount of time. Pop quizzes are given after an unspecified amount of time. Choice (B) is incorrect because *ratio* means a specific number of times someone has to do something in order to be rewarded. In terms of pop quizzes a student cannot do anything to make a pop quiz happen any sooner or later; it is simply an interval of time. *Fixed ratio* means a person has to do something a certain number of specified times to be rewarded, for example, getting paid on commission. *Fixed interval* is a set amount of time between reinforcement, for example, a midterm exam.

135. (B) Extinction is the reduction in a response when the conditioned stimulus is no longer followed by the unconditioned stimulus. As a result, the conditioned stimulus tends to no longer elicit the conditioned response. In this case if the bell is no longer paired with the food, eventually the dogs will stop salivating at the sound of the bell.

136. (D) The unconditioned stimulus is some stimulus that triggers or elicits a physiological reflex, such as fear. In this case Little Albert automatically had a fear response after hearing the loud noise, which makes it the unconditioned stimulus.

137. (A) Because a stimulus must produce a response and not the other way around, choices (B), (C), and (E) can all be eliminated. Choice (D) is incorrect because a conditioned stimulus must produce a conditioned response. Conditioned stimulus means that the stimulus was formerly neutral; therefore, the response is elicited from the conditioned stimulus and called the conditioned response. That leaves choice (A). The UCS produces the UCR.

138. (B) The sailor's hat was a formerly neutral stimulus. Now Dylan has made an association between the sailor's hat and feeling nauseated. The sailor's hat is therefore the conditioned stimulus.

139. (D) Variable ratio is correct because when fishing, a person does not know when or how long it is going to take to catch a fish. Variable interval is incorrect because *interval* simply means "time." Although fishing does take time, you have to do something to catch a fish, such as putting the fishing rod in the water.

140. (C) *Fixed ratio* applies to any job that works on commission. *Ratio* means the number of times you do something to get rewarded. *Fixed* means a set number of times you do something to get rewarded. When people work on commission they know how much merchandise they have to sell in order to get paid.

141. (A) The UCS is a stimulus that triggers or elicits a physiological reflex. In this case, it is the job interview, because it automatically made him nervous. The UCR is unlearned and innate. In this case feeling anxious is a direct, involuntary response to the job interview. The CS is a formerly neutral stimulus. In this case prior to the job interview, the passenger was never afraid to fly. The CR is elicited from the CS; in this case, feeling anxious and nervous about flying would be the CR.

142. **(B)** Prior to the injection of the drug that weakens mice's immune system, the saccharine-flavored water had no effect. Once paired with the injection, the saccharine-flavored water had the same effect.

143. **(D)** The unconditioned response for this advertisement is the desire to buy the car after looking at attractive women with the cars long enough that the mere sight of the car (CS) will elicit a response to buy the car.

144. **(B)** Because the unconditioned stimulus is a stimulus that elicits an involuntary response, the advertisers intentionally placed attractive women in their ads knowing that that would elicit a desire to buy a car.

145. **(C)** Choice (C) is the definition of classical conditioning. The other choices do not include the formerly neutral stimulus, which is what classical conditioning is all about.

146. **(A)** Until paired with the food, the bell did not elicit a response of salivation. Therefore, the bell is the CS. The food automatically made the dogs salivate; therefore, it is the UCS.

147. **(E)** Choice (E) is the definition of desensitization therapy. Choice (D) sounds like it could also be the correct choice, but desensitization therapy does not use the concept of generalization.

148. **(C)** Because classical conditioning has to do with a stimulus and response, choice (C) has to be the correct answer. Choice (A) has to do with operant conditioning. Choices (B), (D), and (E) all have to do with social cognitive learning.

149. **(D)** Choice (D) is the only one that has to do with learned behavior. Choices (A) and (B) are both related to natural physiological occurrences in the body. Choices (C) and (E) are both related to innate behavior.

150. **(B)** Choice (B) uses the term *unconditioned association,* which is directly related to classical conditioning. The other choices do not specifically discuss a stimulus and a response.

Chapter 9: Operant Conditioning and Cognitive Learning

151. **(A)** Operant conditioning is a kind of learning in which a behavior is performed, followed by a consequence. Learning takes place as a result of some voluntary action by the learner. In classical conditioning, learning takes place without choice. The stimulus causes the response. Choice (B) is incorrect because it is actually the opposite. Operant conditioning takes place after the response, while classical conditioning takes place before the response. Choice (C) is also the opposite. Classical conditioning is learning by association, and operant conditioning is learning by reinforcement. Choices (D) and (E) are completely incorrect. Classical conditioning is not part of social cognitive learning.

152. (C) Very often students get confused between negative reinforcement and punishment. Negative reinforcement occurs when something unpleasant is taken away if the subject does something. It is conditional. Punishment is not the same as negative reinforcement. It is an attempt to weaken a response, or a behavior, by following it with something unpleasant. It is not conditional. Because the basketball player should not commit flagrant fouls, he was suspended; therefore, it is a punishment.

153. (B) In this scenario the defendant is harassed until he confesses. The harassment is something unpleasant and it will be taken away once the confession is given, making it negative reinforcement and not punishment.

154. (C) Remember, punishment is an attempt to stop an unwanted behavior. It is not contingent upon a person doing the correct behavior.

155. (D) The law of effect says that if a random act is followed by a pleasurable consequence, such actions are strengthened and will likely occur again. Choice (D) is the definition of the law of effect.

156. (E) Shaping is a procedure in which the experimenter successively reinforces behaviors that lead up to the desired behavior. Many students get confused between shaping and chaining. Chaining is an instructional procedure that involves reinforcing responses in a sequence to form a more complex behavior. In terms of the Skinner box, B. F. Skinner used shaping to condition his rats to press the lever.

157. (B) Variable interval refers to an unknown amount of time, more or less waiting for a desired response to occur. Because it does not matter how many times you pick up the phone to call your friend, the correct answer is variable interval and not variable ratio. Ratio refers to the number of desired acts required before reinforcement will occur.

158. (D) Once the mother takes an aspirin, the unpleasantness of the headache will go away. Choices (A), (B), (C), and (E) are all examples of punishment.

159. (A) Because operant conditioning is learning by reinforcement, which takes place after the response, choice (A) has to be the correct answer. None of the other choices have anything to do with the principles of operant conditioning.

160. (B) Positive reinforcement occurs when something the subject wants is added to encourage the wanted behavior to continue. Negative reinforcement occurs when something unpleasant is taken away once the wanted behavior continues. Both have the same goal, to repeat wanted behavior.

161. (B) Choice (B) is the definition of latent learning. Often humans and animals need motivation or good reason to show their behavior, which does not mean they have not learned the behavior. Choice (A) can apply to almost any form of learning. Choice (D) defines operant conditioning. Choice (E) can sound similar, but latent learning does not say the actual learning occurs after the behavior, just the demonstration of the learning.

162. (C) Edward Tolman's theory of latent learning suggested that the concept of response needed to include a range of behaviors that would allow learners to reach their goals. Tolman felt that learning usually occurs before the goal is reached.

163. (D) A cognitive map is a learned mental image of a spatial environment. This image is usually learned without the learner realizing he or she has learned it. Choice (D) is the only answer that suggests this.

164. (A) Insight is learning that occurs rapidly based on understanding all the elements of a problem. In this case, the chimps learned how to obtain the banana shortly after figuring out their environment.

165. (E) A learning set is the ability to become increasingly more effective in solving problems the more practice you have. In this case the monkeys learned how to choose the correct box based on their problem-solving techniques used with each trial. Based on this idea, *learning sets* really means learning how to learn.

166. (B) Social cognitive learning emphasizes the ability to learn by observation without firsthand experience. It does not specify that a person must observe rewarded behavior. Choice (D) can be confused for the correct answer, but it is too vague when the question is asking which statement best exemplifies social cognitive learning.

167. (A) In the Albert Bandura "bobo" doll experiment, the children who watched the video in which a person was rewarded for acting violently toward the doll were first to act aggressively. Although after being offered candy by the experimenter, children from all of the groups did demonstrate aggressive behavior, initially it was the model-reward condition.

168. (C) Vicarious learning, or observational learning, is simply learning by observing other people, as Devyn did in this scenario.

169. (E) Albert Bandura is the most prominent proponent of social cognitive learning, which emphasizes learning through observation. Tolman studied latent learning. Kohler studied insight learning. B. F. Skinner studied operant conditioning. Watson studied classical conditioning.

170. (D) Choice (D) is the only behavior that is innate. Although toddlers do get positive reinforcement when they begin to walk, it would happen with or without the reinforcement.

171. (E) The Premack Principle states that more probable behaviors will reinforce less probable behaviors. In this case it is that Joey will respond with correct behavior when using trains. Applying this reinforcement to get him to complete his homework could work, according to this principle.

172. (B) Insight learning occurs rapidly as a result of understanding all of the elements of a problem. In this case, Spencer suddenly arrived at the answer after working out the elements of the math problem. Choice (A) refers to learning that is not immediately reflected in the behavior. Choice (C) is simply learning how to learn. Choice (D) is vague and incorrect. Choice (E) is learning based on reward and punishment.

173. (D) Learned helplessness is defined as failure to take steps to avoid or escape from an aversive stimulus that occurs as a result of previous unavoidable painful stimuli. The dogs, having no way out for several minutes, gave up, even when there was a viable escape.

174. (B) Spontaneous recovery is the reappearance of an extinguished response after some time has passed. In this case, Jada's fear of going to the dentist returned only when she had to go back for a root canal. That is an example of spontaneous recovery. Generalization would have been if Jada feared all doctors as a result of her fear of the dentist.

175. (A) Money is an example of a primary reinforcer.

Chapter 10: Memory

176. (C) Encoding is the process of transferring information from short-term memory to long-term memory by paying attention to it or by forming new associations. In this case Katie made a new association with the number 111. Choice (D) does seem like it could be the correct answer because it is the ability to retain information; however, encoding gives a more specific explanation.

177. (A) Episodic memory is a type of memory that involves knowledge of a specific event or personal experience. In this case, remembering that you got a bicycle is a personal memory. Choices (B), (D), and (E) are all examples of semantic memory. Choice (C) is an example of procedural memory.

178. (C) Procedural memory involves things learned through classical conditioning. We are not aware of these memories and cannot retrieve them. In this case Sophia is unable to explain her fear of spiders, which would fall under procedural memories.

179. (D) The hippocampus transfers words, facts, and personal events from short-term memory to long-term memory. People with damage to the hippocampus cannot save any declarative memories. Choice (C) could be tempting, but the amygdala deals with emotional feelings associated with memories, not the transfer from STM to LTM.

180. (B) Echoic memory is a form of sensory memory that holds auditory information for one to two seconds. In this case you are able to recall your friend's exact words because they are still in your echoic memory. Iconic memory is a form of sensory memory that holds visual information for a brief period of time. Sensory memory is the initial process that receives and holds environmental information. Short-term memory is the process of holding information for a short period of time, but it is not what would have been used in this particular situation.

181. (E) For information to be processed it must go through three steps: Encoding using sensory receptors is the initial step because it is picking up information from the environment in its raw form. Storing information is the second step in the process; to retrieve the information at a later time, the information has to be stored properly to begin with. The third step is the ability, when necessary, to retrieve it. Information cannot be retrieved before it has been stored.

182. (E) The only false statement is choice (E). Procedural memory involves skills, habits, and things learned through classical conditioning, not declarative memory. Declarative memory involves facts or events such as scenes, stories, words, or conversations.

183. (D) State-dependent learning is the idea that we recall information more easily when we are in the same physiological or emotional state as when the information was originally encoded. In this case when Jeff drank alcohol, it put him in the same physiological state, enabling him to remember the details of the crime.

184. (B) Short-term memory is called working memory because it can hold only a limited amount of information for a short period of time, between 2 and 30 seconds. If during that time you become more involved in the information, it can last longer.

185. (C) Eidetic memory or imagery is the ability to examine a picture and then retain the detailed visual image. This is found in a small percentage of children. Flashbulb memories are vivid recollections of dramatic incidents. Semantic memories are declarative memories consisting of factual knowledge. Echoic memories hold auditory information. Iconic memories hold visual images.

186. (A) The amygdala is responsible for emotionally charged memories.

187. (B) Choice (B) specifically describes the phenomenon behind the primacy effect. Words at the beginning of a list are more likely to be remembered because of proper rehearsal and encoding techniques. Choices (C) and (E) would apply to the recency effect.

188. (D) Semantic memory involves knowledge of facts, concepts, words, definitions, and language rules. Episodic memory is incorrect because it involves specific personal experiences. Procedural memory is incorrect because it involves memories of skills and habits.

189. (A) Long-term memory does have an unlimited capacity. Short-term memory can hold an average of seven items for up to 30 seconds. The other choices were simply put there to confuse the reader.

190. (B) Choice (B) is the definition of maintenance rehearsal. Intentionally repeating information can help the information remain in your short-term memory for a longer period of time.

191. (A) Short-term memory is also called working memory for this very reason. Because it only has a limited amount of space, one must make a conscious effort to keep the information there for a short period of time before it disappears. The other choices do not apply to the scenario.

192. (D) Chunking is combining separate items of information into a larger unit, then remembering chunks of information rather than individual items. Elaborate rehearsal involves actively making meaningful associations between information, not what was done in the scenario presented in the question. Maintenance rehearsal is simply repeating information.

193. (B) Making associations increases the likelihood that the information will be encoded properly. Repetition by itself does not ensure efficient encoding from STM to LTM.

194. (C) Maintenance rehearsal, the practice of intentionally repeating information, is necessary for information to remain in STM for up to 30 seconds. For information to be processed into LTM, elaborate rehearsal is necessary. Elaborate rehearsal involves making meaningful associations between information to be learned and information already stored in long-term memory.

195. (D) Chunking is the only choice that is not part of effortful encoding. Effortful encoding involves the transfer of information from STM to LTM either by repeating the information, rehearsing it, or making associations between new and old information.

Chapter 11: Remembering and Forgetting

196. (B) Eyewitness testimony refers to recalling or recognizing a suspect observed during a potentially disrupting emotional situation. Because of the concern of eyewitness testimony, studies have been conducted to show that people can be misled, especially if given false information. Furthermore, asking a person misleading questions can create false memories.

197. (C) This is a simple definition answer. Nodes are memory files. Schemas are not memory files but mental categories, which is why choice (E) can be confusing.

198. (D) The forgetting curve measures the amount of previously learned information that the subject can recall or recognize over time. Ebbinghaus himself forgot the greatest number of nonsense syllables within the first hour.

199. (B) Proactive interference occurs when old information, in this case the Spanish language, blocks or disrupts the remembering of related new information, in this case, the Italian language. Choice (A) is not correct because retroactive interference occurs when new information blocks the retrieval of old information learned earlier. Choices (C) and (D) refer to a type of amnesia that occurs after a head trauma.

200. (C) Retrograde amnesia involves memory loss for events that occurred before the time of the head trauma. Choice (A) is the definition for anterograde amnesia. The other choices do not apply to this question.

201. (E) Suppression is the process of deliberately trying to stop thinking about something. Repression is the unconscious process of forgetting past memories. Amnesia is usually brought on by some type of head trauma. Forgetting is the inability to retrieve, recall, or recognize information.

202. (B) Anterograde amnesia is the type of amnesia that prevents an individual from making new memories after the head trauma. Retrograde amnesia is the inability to recall events preceding the head trauma. Choices (C) and (D) refer to blocking or disrupting information.

203. (C) The method of loci is an encoding technique that creates visual associations between already memorized places and new items to be memorized. It is a three-step process that involves memorizing familiar places, creating associations for each item to be memorized, and putting each item into the memorized place. An example of this could be selecting a specific place in your apartment to keep your keys and always remembering that place. Based on this definition, choice (C) is the correct answer.

204. (D) The hippocampus works similar to the save button on your computer. It transfers a file into permanent storage on your hard drive. People with damage to the hippocampus cannot save any declarative memories, such as new words or personal events.

205. (B) Rote rehearsal is also known as maintenance rehearsal. It is the practice of intentionally repeating information so it remains longer in short-term memory. Elaborate rehearsal involves actively making meaningful associations between information to be learned and information already stored in long-term memory.

206. (C) The decay theory argues that the passage of time causes forgetting. In this case, the passage of time caused the subjects to forget the three letters. Choices (A) and (B) refer to the disruption of information due to either new information or old information getting in the way. The forgetting curve is probably the choice most students will mistake for the correct answer. But the forgetting curve is based on the idea that the majority of information is forgotten within the first hour and then it levels off. This question does not give enough information for the reader to assume the forgetting curve phenomenon was at work here.

207. (B) Remember, retrograde interference is when new information disrupts the retrieval of old information. In this case Ava studied the bones in the foot, the new information, which interfered with remembering the bones in the hand, the old information. Choice (A) is an example of proactive interference.

208. (D) Implicit memory is information that either was unintentionally committed to memory or was unintentionally retrieved from memory. In this case, Jack did not realize he remembered where a particular piece of information was on a page; therefore, it is an example of implicit memory. Explicit memory is intentionally committing information to memory.

209. (B) Recognition involves identifying previously learned information with the help of more external cues. A multiple-choice test is an example of recognition. Choice (A) is an example of recall, not recognition. Choice (D) was placed there to confuse students. Recognition is not creating entirely new responses.

210. (D) Recall involves retrieving previously learned information, in this case, items from the grocery store, without the aid of or with very few external cues.

211. (A) The method of loci creates a visual association between already memorized places and new items to be memorized. In this scenario, the playroom is the "already memorized place." The toys are the "to be memorized items." The peg method refers to an encoding process that creates associations between number-word rhymes and items to be memorized, for example, "one is thumb, two is shoe."

212. (B) Herman Ebbinghaus's research showed that the greatest number of nonsense syllables were forgotten within the first hour. Afterward the amount of information forgotten levels off.

213. (A) Choice (A) is the definition of the forgetting curve.

214. (C) Recognition involves identifying previously learned information with the help of external cues. Multiple-choice questions exemplify recognition because cues exist. Recall involves retrieving previously learned information without the aid of external cues. A fill-in-the-blank test does not give the reader any cues to work with.

215. (A) Repression is a mental process that involves automatically hiding emotionally threatening or anxiety-provoking information in the unconscious. In this scenario, Kimberly did something embarrassing and her unconscious is blocking her memory of the event.

Chapter 12: Intelligence and Testing

216. (A) Mental age is defined as an estimation of a child's intellectual ability, based on his or her score on an intelligence test. Choices (B) and (C) were put there to throw off the test taker. Neither raw score nor computed age have anything to do with mental age. Choice (D) mentions child's age level, which is another concept used to throw off the reader. Choice (E), charting a child's age, does not make clear enough sense to be the correct answer.

217. (B) Validity means the test is measuring what it is supposed to. A test with little or no validity produces results that could be produced by guessing or by chance. Choice (A) might confuse some students. A reliable test refers to the consistency: a person's score on a test at one point in time should be similar to the score obtained by the same person on a similar test at another point in time. Choice (D) refers to the test conditions, which should remain constant for all students taking the exam.

218. (C) Alfred Binet, best known as the father of intelligence, believed strongly that intelligence was a collection of mental abilities and that the best way to assess intelligence was to measure a person's ability to perform cognitive tasks. Paul Broca, a neurologist, claimed that there was a considerable relationship between size of the brain and intelligence. This later proved to be unreliable and poorly correlated. David Wechsler created both the WISC and the WAIS, both of which focused on performance-based IQ tests to eliminate cultural bias. Lewis Terman, in 1916, devised a formula to calculate an intelligence quotient score. Francis Galton observed that intelligent people often had intelligent relatives and concluded that intelligence is, to a large extent, inherited.

219. (D) Reaction range indicates the extent to which traits, abilities, and IQ scores vary as a result of environmental interactions. For example, one's IQ score can vary as much as 10 to 15 points depending on whether one has an enriched, normal, or impoverished environment. Students may confuse the correct answer for choice (B), heritability, which is the number that indicates the amount of some ability or trait that can be attributed to genetic factors.

220. (D) The calculation for the intelligence quotient is MA/CA × 100. In this case the MA is 5 and the CA is 4: 5/4 = 1.25; 1.25 × 100 = 125.

221. (A) The most widely used IQ tests are the Wechsler Adult Intelligence Scale for ages 16 and older and the Wechsler Intelligence Scale for Children for ages 3 to 16. The test includes a verbal and a performance section. The performance section contains a subtest that involves arranging pictures and assembling objects. The test was designed to eliminate any cultural biases by using nontraditional methods of testing.

222. (C) Spearman's two-factor theory says that intelligence has a general mental ability, which represents what different cognitive tasks have in common, as well as specific factors, which include mathematical and verbal skills.

223. (E) Sternberg's triarchic theory says that intelligence can be divided into three ways of gathering information: (1) Analytical thinking skills are measured by traditional intelligence tests. (2) Problem-solving skills require creative thinking and learning from experience. (3) Practical thinking skills help a person adjust and cope with his or her environment.

224. (B) Crystallized intelligence is the ability to retain information, while fluid intelligence refers to the ability to solve problems.

225. (A) Howard Gardner's theory is called the theory of multiple intelligence. Gardner proposes eight different types of intelligence: linguistic, logical-mathematical, musical, spatial, body-kinesthetic, interpersonal, intrapersonal, and naturalistic. Choice (C), Louis Thurstone, believed there was an existence of a wider range of components of intelligence, specifically eight primary mental abilities. But the ones mentioned in the question refer to Gardner's theory and not Thurstone's theory.

226. (A) A score of 85 places you one standard deviation below the mean. In a perfectly normal distribution, that means you have outperformed about 16 percent of the other test takers.

227. (B) Aptitude measures the capacity of the test taker to perform some task in the future. Choice (A) could look like the correct answer, but achievement measures an individual's knowledge of a particular subject.

228. (C) Savants are individuals, not necessarily children, with serious cognitive limitations such as mental retardation or autism who possess a remarkable talent in art or music. This eliminates choices (A), (B), (D), and (E).

229. (E) Charles Spearman's concept of "g," or general intelligence, is a unitary reference to a sort of overall smartness, which does not suggest the existence of more than one kind of intelligence.

230. (A) This is a definition question. An IQ of 55–70 is mild retardation, 40–55 is moderate retardation, 25–40 is severe retardation, and below 25 is profound retardation.

231. **(B)** David Wechsler created both tests to eliminate cultural biases that exist in IQ testing by adding a performance component to his test. WAIS stands for the Wechsler Adult Intelligence Scale, and the WISC is the Wechsler Intelligence Scale for Children.

232. **(D)** The MMPI was originally designed to diagnose mental disorders, and it is still widely used as an assessment tool among clinicians. It has more than 500 true-or-false items designed to identify characteristics of personality and behavior.

233. **(C)** Projective tests of personality want the subject's impression of ambiguous stimuli. The Rorschach test offers an array of inkblots for subjects to identify. On the Myers-Briggs Type Indicator test you are asked to choose which statement is most representative of your own thoughts.

234. **(D)** This is the definition of equivalent reliability. Choice (A) is the definition for the split half reliability. Choice (B) could be confused as the correct answer, but reliability measures standardized tests only. Choice (C) is the definition for inter-rater reliability.

235. **(A)** Choices (B), (C), and (D) can all be eliminated because Binet did not come up with the intelligence quotient; Lewis Terman did. Choice (E) is incorrect because Binet did not become the father of intelligence by discussing heritability.

236. **(D)** Studies have shown just how important environment can be to IQ scores, eliminating choices (A), (B), and (E). Data also shows that an IQ can change by 10 to 15 points.

237. **(B)** Reaction range indicates the extent to which certain factors or abilities increase or decrease as a result of the environment. Although choice (C) may sound correct, reaction range does not say intelligence is completely due to environmental factors.

238. **(A)** In terms of genetics, fraternal twins are no different from other siblings—unlike identical twins, who share the same genetic material.

239. **(C)** The score of 85 is one standard deviation below the average. The score of 115 is one standard deviation above the average. This means that in a normal distribution curve the percentage is 68.26 percent.

240. **(D)** To know this answer you must study a distribution curve. In this case knowing the curve would tell you only choice (D) could be correct.

Chapter 13: Thought and Language

241. **(C)** The prototype theory says that a person forms a concept by creating a mental image that is based on the average characteristics of an object. To identify new objects the person matches it to the one for which he or she has already formed a prototype. In this case a poodle has four legs, average size, with nose, tail, and ears. Therefore it would be a prototype.

242. (D) Functional fixedness refers to a mental set that is characterized by the inability to see an object as having a function different from its usual one.

243. (A) An algorithm is a fixed set of rules that, if followed correctly, will eventually lead to a solution. Because this holds true for chess or checkers, (A) is the correct answer. A heuristic is a shortcut, allowing one to solve a problem more easily. A concept is a way to group objects. A prototype is the average characteristic of an object. Morphemes are the smallest meaningful combination of sounds.

244. (B) Availability heuristic says that we rely on information that is most prominent or easily recalled and overlook other information that is available but less prominent. In this case, students might choose (A), representative heuristic, but representative heuristic is similar to a stereotype, not prominent information.

245. (C) Convergent thinkers begin with a problem and come up with a single correct answer, while divergent thinkers begin with a problem and come up with many different solutions. Because an algorithm is a fixed set of rules, it is more likely used among convergent thinkers.

246. (D) Representative heuristic is problem solving based on stereotyping. In this case, Janet was stereotyping pilots by assuming the pilot was a male. Confirmation bias is incorrect because it means ignoring all information that does not support your beliefs. Janet was not ignoring anything; instead she was assuming. Convergent thinking is incorrect because Janet is not coming up with one solution to solve her problem. Availability heuristic is incorrect because Janet is not basing her answer on the most prominent information.

247. (B) Phonemes are the basic sounds of consonants and vowels.

248. (E) Noam Chomsky's theory states that all languages share a universal grammar and that all children inherit a mental program to learn this universal grammar.

249. (A) Chomsky is the only choice who believes language development is innate. Whorf believes culture influences language. Skinner is a behaviorist. Saffron is not a psychologist whom students would need to know for the exam. Sapir worked with Whorf on his language theory.

250. (C) Choice (C) is the only choice that states language development is innate. The other choices all support the Whorf-Sapir linguistic relativity hypothesis, which states that culture has a direct influence on determining the words that become part of our language.

251. (D) Confirmation bias is the tendency to find information that supports one's beliefs and ignore information that refutes them. This can sometimes prevent problem solving.

252. (B) A compensatory model is a rational decision-making model in which choices are systematically evaluated on various criteria. In this case the attractive features can offset or compensate for the unattractive features. Choice (C) can be confusing. The noncompensatory model is a decision-making model in which weakness in one or more criteria are not offset by strengths in other criteria.

253. (A) Overregularization is when children apply grammatical rules without making appropriate exceptions. In this case "I goed to the store" indicates the use of the general rule that we form the past tense by adding "-ed" to the word.

254. (D) Noam Chomsky believes that children are born with a language acquisition device, an internal mechanism for processing speech, wired into the human brain.

255. (D) A holophrase is a one-word sentence, commonly used by children under two years of age to represent a larger, more meaningful concept.

256. (A) Framing refers to the way an issue is stated. How an issue is framed can affect a person's perception or decision. In this case women were more likely to go get a mammogram after hearing they could die if they didn't, rather than that it could save their life.

257. (B) This is the definition of the term *babbling.*

258. (A) Language stages refer to four different forms: phonemes, morphemes, syntax, and semantics. Easier to understand are the four stages: babbling, one-word phrase, two-word combinations, and sentences.

259. (E) All of the other choices give examples of thinking outside the box and seeing a way to use an object besides its true purpose. Choice (E), the math formula, does not apply to functional fixedness.

260. (A) The definition theory is the idea that we form a concept of an object by making a mental list of the actual or essential properties that define it.

261. (C) Availability heuristic is a general rule by which we rely on information that is more prominent and easily recalled and overlook other information that is less prominent. In this case, Steven complains about his job after having a bad day and overlooks the fact that he really does enjoy his job.

262. (C) Information retrieval is a problem-solving strategy that requires only the recovery of information from long-term memory. In this scenario, information retrieval is an important option when a solution must be found quickly. This is why choice (A), remembering a 16th birthday, is not the correct answer.

263. (E) Solving an anagram by trying every possible letter guarantees a solution. Therefore, this is an example of an algorithm.

264. (A) Functional fixedness is not a problem-solving strategy. It is a mental set characterized by the inability to see an object having multiple uses, different from its usual one.

265. (B) This is a definition question. Subgoals involve creating separate parts. Brainstorming involves coming up with various solutions, heuristics are shortcuts to problem solving, and algorithms are fixed sets of rules.

Chapter 14: Motivation

266. (B) Choice (B) is the definition of motivation. The other choices do not correctly define motivation. Choice (A) defines fixed action pattern. Choice (C) defines a need. Choice (D) defines homeostasis. Choice (E) defines incentives.

267. (C) Instincts are innate tendencies or biological forces. The examples given are all innate feelings. Many students might look at choice (B) as the correct answer; however, emotions include subjective feelings. Instincts occur without subjectivity.

268. (D) The drive reduction theory says that a need results in a drive, creating a state of tension. A person must act to reduce that state of tension and return to homeostasis.

269. (C) A fixed action pattern is an innate biological force that predisposes an organism to behave in a fixed way in a specific environmental condition. In this case, the baboon is innately reacting to a condition in his environment, for survival. Choices (A) and (B) refer to needs. Needs are not innate patterns of behavior. Choices (D) and (E) are examples of conditioning.

270. (A) Intrinsic motivation involves behaviors that are personally rewarding and help us fulfill our beliefs. The other choices are examples of extrinsic motivation and positive reinforcement.

271. (C) According to Maslow's hierarchy of needs, level 3 is love and belonging—which simply means affiliation with others.

272. (E) According to Maslow's hierarchy of needs, level 5 is self-actualization. Self-actualization is the fulfillment of one's unique potential. This involves developing and reaching our full potential as a unique individual.

273. (B) Esteem needs refer to achievement competency and gaining approval. In this case, earning a master's degree would be an example of achievement.

274. (B) The lateral hypothalamus regulates hunger by creating feelings of being hungry. The other choices are all examples of satiety signals.

275. (B) Choice (B) is the definition of homeostasis. Once a need is satisfied, the body will return to a state of equilibrium.

276. (D) The ventromedial hypothalamus regulates hunger by creating a feeling of satiety. Therefore, if the ventromedial hypothalamus is destroyed, the feeling of satiety will go away, causing the organism to overeat.

277. (E) Set point is a certain level of body fat our bodies try to maintain throughout our lives. When an individual's set point is high, so is his or her fat storage and body fat.

278. (A) The metabolic rate refers to how efficiently our body breaks down food into energy and how quickly our bodies burn it off. If a person has a low metabolic rate he or she will burn less fuel and store more fuel as fat, thus having a fatter body.

279. (E) Nutrition is the only choice that does not involve psychology. To put it another way, choices (A), (B), (C), and (D) all deal with issues other than physiological changes in the body.

280. (C) Gender identity differs from gender role in that gender identity is a subjective feeling about being male or female. Gender roles are stereotypical attitudes society designates as feminine or masculine.

281. (B) Gender roles are traditional attitudes society designates to both females and males. By age five, for example, boys learn stereotypical male behavior like playing sports. Girls learn the importance of physical appearance.

282. (B) The lateral hypothalamus signals hunger, while the ventromedial hypothalamus signals satiety.

283. (D) Maslow's hierarchy of needs demonstrates the importance of the order in which you satisfy your biological and social needs. Biological needs must be met first. If you are starving and homeless you cannot worry about earning a master's degree.

284. (B) The incentive theory refers to environmental factors, such as external stimuli, reinforcers, or rewards that motivate a person to behave in a certain way. In this case the journalist was looking for recognition and the ability to increase his or her salary, both incentives based on external stimuli.

285. (C) Motivational behavior starts with a biological state in which an organism lacks something essential in its life. The need produces a drive, which in turn motivates action.

Chapter 15: Emotion

286. (B) Because the James-Lange theory focuses on the interpretation of physiological changes in the body, only choice (A) or (B) can be the correct answer. In this case, choice (B) is correct because in order to feel an emotion, according to the James-Lange theory, one must interpret the physiological change first before having the emotion.

287. (A) The facial feedback theory says that your brain interprets the sensations or feedback from the movement of your face muscles. This idea originated with Charles Darwin as a means of survival.

288. (C) James and Lange believed that our interpretation of our physiological changes in the body determine the emotions we are feeling. The problem with this theory is that many different emotions share the same physiological changes in the body. Therefore, physiological changes are not specific enough to determine emotions.

289. **(D)** Schachter and Singer conducted an experiment in which subjects were injected with adrenaline, causing increased heart rate and blood pressure. Half the subjects were placed in a room with an extremely happy person and the other half were placed in the room with an extremely angry person. Those in the room with the happy person associated their physiological changes with that person. Those in the room with the angry person associated their physiological changes with that person. These results helped to prove the Schachter-Singer theory, that perception is everything.

290. **(A)** Choice (A) is the only one that is based on a person's interpretation or perception of the situation before feeling an emotion.

291. **(D)** The affective-primacy theory states that in some situations you can feel an emotion before having the time to interpret the situation. An example could be as follows: you are walking in a forest, you hear leaves rustling behind you, and you feel scared before you have time to assess the situation.

292. **(B)** Researchers Ekman and Friesen concluded that there is evidence for innately determined universal facial emotional expressions. The evidence came from studying people's recognition of emotional expressions in remote areas of the world.

293. **(A)** The fact that infants show fear, universally between the ages of five and seven months, is proof that emotional expressions are innate. The other choices are based on modeling, which does not support the Ekman-Friesen experiment.

294. **(C)** According to the Yerkes-Dodson law, performance on a task depends on the level of physiological arousal and the difficulty of the task. Low arousal is better for success on a difficult task. High arousal can help on the performance of easy tasks.

295. **(D)** Studies have shown that an individual's happiness is based more on positive feelings and overall life satisfaction than on the amount of money one makes.

296. **(A)** The adaptation level theory states that a person can quickly become comfortable receiving a large fortune and begin to take it for granted. Eventually this contributes less to long-term levels of happiness. The Yerkes-Dodson law has to do with physiological arousal and difficulty of task. The relative deprivation theory has to do with a sense of entitlement for others.

297. **(D)** According to display rules, individual cultures determine appropriate emotional expression. Choices (B) and (C) can look like the correct answer but, again, they both depend on cultural attitudes and are, therefore, really part of choice (D).

298. **(E)** The cognitive-appraisal theory assumes that your appraisal of a situation is often the primary cause of emotion. Choice (A), the affective-primacy theory, focuses on emotion before interpretation. Choices (B), (C), and (D) all focus on how physiological change influences our interpretation, not subjective feelings.

299. (B) Schachter and Singer believed that thoughts are important in establishing an emotional feeling. Based on the scenario, this belief would hold true and actually goes against the ideas behind the other choices.

300. (C) Cannon and Bard believed that physiological changes and the brain's interpretation happen at the same time. Although the James-Lange theory stated physiological changes happen first, Cannon and Bard believed that it is not one before the other. Instead, they occur at the same time.

301. (A) The cognitive-appraisal theory is the only one of these choices that focuses on subjectivity of an emotional experience based on the situation.

302. (B) The James-Lange theory said that physiological changes in the body determine the interpretation of an emotion. Therefore, we cry and then we know we are sad. The Cannon-Bard theory stated that those two occurrences happen simultaneously. The facial feedback theory focuses on facial muscle movement.

303. (B) Approach-avoidance conflict is a conflict that has one positive consequence and one negative consequence, unlike approach-approach conflict, which has two positive consequences.

304. (C) Because Latoya must choose between two excellent colleges, it has two positive consequences.

305. (D) The limbic system controls a large amount of our emotional stability.

306. (C) The opponent-process theory of emotion states that eventually our level of emotion changes with experience.

307. (E) Robert Zajonc believed that feelings or emotions might occur before thinking. This thinking is part of the affective-primacy theory. Choices (B), (C), and (D) all agree that interpretation occurs before the emotion.

308. (A) The hypothalamus deals with feeling and having emotional responses. The thalamus is the brain's "switchboard." The temporal lobe deals with auditory control. The parietal lobe deals with the sensation of touch. The amygdala controls emotional memories.

309. (A) The adaptation level theory states that we quickly become accustomed to receiving a new fortune and eventually take it for granted. This is why choice (A) is the correct answer. The other choices do not refer to taking anything for granted.

310. (A) The Yerkes-Dodson law states that difficult tasks are more successful with low arousal and easy tasks are performed better with high arousal. Because simple tasks can be boring, high arousal can keep the person from becoming disengaged.

Chapter 16: Developmental Psychology: Infancy and Childhood

311. (A) Cross-sectional research is a research method used by developmental psychologists because it uses several groups of different-aged individuals who are studied at the same time, saving time and money. Longitudinal research studies the same group of individuals repeatedly at many different points of time.

312. (B) Developmental psychology focuses on the idea that while there are many common patterns to human development, each person's development is also in some ways unique. The combination of shared and distinctive elements is characteristic of all human development. The second theme stresses stability and change. Human development is characterized by both major life transitions and continuities.

313. (E) Choices (A), (B), (C), and (D) are all examples of reflexes that babies are born with. Choice (E), licking, is not considered to be an innate reflex.

314. (C) Temperament, like personality, is described as the characteristics of a newborn child. Infant temperament has been put into three categories: easy, difficult, and slow-to-warm-up babies. Choice (A) is incorrect because temperament is not necessarily inherited from parents. Choice (B) is incorrect because children are born with a certain temperament; it is not learned. Choice (D) is incorrect because temperament is not modeled behavior. Choice (E) is incorrect because children do not necessarily outgrow temperament.

315. (D) The key word in this question is *all*. The other choices would be correct if the question said "some children." Between 6 and 12 months all babies do acquire depth perception.

316. (A) Choice (A) is the definition of proximodistal. *Proximo* in Latin means "near," and *distal* means "far."

317. (C) Choice (C) is the definition of maturation. Maturation is a biological process, therefore eliminating choices (A) and (D). Choices (B) and (E) are too vague to clearly define the term.

318. (E) Many students might get confused with choice (D), but the question asks at which stage children are able to grasp the concept of conservation. That would make choice (E) correct. It is during the concrete-operational stage that children are able to grasp those principles.

319. (B) When talking about egocentrism, Piaget believed this concept dealt with preschool-age children. At that age, he believed children do not see things from a different point of view than their own.

320. (A) This stage of cognitive development is usually reached during adolescence. Individuals begin to think in abstract terms. They become capable of going beyond the here and now to understand things in terms of cause and effect.

321. (C) Object permanence, according to Piaget, is grasped during the sensorimotor stage of development. It is an awareness that objects exist when they are out of sight. By the time children are between 18 and 24 months old, they can imagine the movement of an object they do not see move.

322. (B) Symbolism is the idea that children can understand that symbols or small objects represent something larger in real life. Children, according to Piaget, can grasp this concept during the preoperational stage, between the ages of two and seven.

323. (A) Depending on age, children assimilate in different ways. An infant sees a block and sucks on it. A toddler sees a block and stacks it or throws it. Adolescents use blocks to play games. Choice (B) could look like the correct answer, but because it only says "thought process," it does not give the exact understanding of the term.

324. (D) According to Lawrence Kohlberg, children in the preconventional stage make decisions based on right or wrong behavior and whether they will be rewarded or punished. Choice (D) uses the term *concrete consequences,* meaning just that.

325. (B) During the conventional stage, adolescents shift their thought process toward considering various abstract social virtues, such as being a good citizen and respecting authority. Some students might get confused with choice (C), postconventional. Postconventional deals more with personal convictions, not necessarily taking into account rules and laws.

326. (C) According to Erik Erikson, during stage 3, initiative versus guilt, a child deals with cognitive development and is expected to meet a new set of challenges. Trust versus mistrust is from birth through the first year of life. Autonomy versus self-doubt is from age one until age three. Industry versus inferiority is from age five through age twelve. Identity versus role confusion is the adolescent years.

327. (D) Autonomy versus self-doubt, according to Erik Erikson, is between the ages of one and three. It is during this time a child is exploring, walking, and talking, thus beginning the battle of wills with his or her parents. With encouragement, a child will gain a sense of independence. With disapproval comes feelings of doubt.

328. (B) The psychosexual stages are five different developmental periods: oral, anal, phallic, latency, and genital. During these stages an individual seeks pleasure from different areas of the body.

329. (E) Both Sigmund Freud and Erik Erikson believed that if individuals do not solve their problems during each psychosexual or psychosocial stage, problems could arise in the next stage of development.

330. (B) Freud believed that if an individual is fixated in the anal stage he or she will continue to engage in behaviors that are related to retention. In this case, overly orderly and stingy are examples of retentive behavior.

331. (A) According to Freud, those individuals fixated in the oral stage can, as adults, become sarcastic and suffer from a low self-esteem, continually looking for approval.

332. (C) According to Lawrence Kohlberg, during the postconventional stage, individuals base their morality on their convictions even if their convictions force them to break the law. Choice (B) could seem like the correct answer, but during the conventional stage, individuals are compelled to follow the law.

333. (D) Choice (A) can be eliminated immediately. Piaget did use different ages for each stage. Choice (B) is incorrect because Piaget was studying cognitive psychology; therefore, he could not have placed too much emphasis on it. Many critics believed Piaget simplified the cognitive abilities of children so much so that he underestimated what they could accomplish.

334. (C) Choice (C) is the definition of rooting.

335. (E) Harry Harlow's work with monkeys and surrogate mothers showed that even monkeys who were deprived of food preferred the terrycloth monkey to the wire monkey with food, demonstrating how important contact and comfort are.

Chapter 17: Developmental Psychology: Adolescence and Adulthood

336. (D) The formal operational stage, Piaget believed, extends from age 11 through adulthood. It is during this stage that adults develop the ability to think abstractly or hypothetically. Adolescents' thoughts about marriage and finding a job in their future is an example of thinking abstractly.

337. (A) Imaginary audience refers to a type of egocentric thinking among teenagers in which they confuse their thoughts with the belief that everyone is staring at them. Choice (B) might seem like the correct answer, but personal fable is the belief among teenagers that their story is unique from anyone else's, that no one could possibly understand them.

338. (B) Personal fable is when a teenager thinks his or her thoughts are unique to him or her. In this scenario Lola believes no one else could understand how in love she is.

339. (D) Authoritative parents try to encourage their children in a rational and intelligent way. They are supportive, loving, and committed. They have a verbal give-and-take with their children and discuss rules and policies together.

340. (A) The identity versus role confusion stage, according to Erikson, is a time when teenagers have to leave behind the carefree and impulsive behaviors of childhood and develop a purposeful planned adulthood. Choices (B), (C), (D), and (E) all reflect later stages in Erikson's psychosocial stages of development.

341. (C) Passion involves constant thoughts about your loved one. Intimacy involves the ability to be completely honest and feeling completely close with your partner. Commitment is making a pledge to maintain the relationship for the long term. Passionate love and companionate love are subcomponents, according to Sternberg.

342. (D) One major criticism of Kohlberg's theory on moral development came from Carol Gilligan. She believed men and women may differ in their moral thinking; men use justice and women use care. Both are socialized differently and, therefore, their moral development will differ greatly.

343. (B) Most psychologists believe that because authoritative parenting involves a give-and-take relationship in which children have a voice, it is the type of parenting that will lead to success in the future.

344. (A) According to Erik Erikson, adolescents are in a stage called identity versus role confusion. Erikson believed that there is a conflict that has to be resolved at every stage in psychosocial development. In this particular stage, if teenagers do not develop an identity they will enter the next stage with role confusion.

345. (B) Many students might feel compelled to choose (C) because the question suggests a reference to the start of preschool. But, in fact, teachers and friends actually become important before preschool. During the initiative versus guilt stage, children are exposed to individuals besides their parents, which is why choice (B) is correct.

346. (D) Similar in many ways to Erik Erikson, Levinson studied the psychosocial stages of male adulthood.

347. (A) During the industry versus inferiority stage, a child must learn to direct his or her energy toward completing tasks. Teenagers begin to understand the value of success, mainly through report card grades.

348. (D) Erik Erikson argued that people in their middle adulthood (40–65) are in the stage generativity versus stagnation. Middle adulthood is a time for helping the younger generation. On the negative side, a lack of involvement leads to feelings of stagnation—doing nothing for the younger generation. Choice (C) refers to young adulthood, and choice (E) refers to late adulthood.

349. (C) According to Lawrence Kohlberg, the postconventional stage represents the highest level of moral reasoning. Moral decisions are made after careful thinking about all alternatives and making a balance between human rights and laws of society. Choice (C) is correct because unlike in Kohlberg's other stages of moral development, in the postconventional stage people decide their behavior based on their own morals and values.

350. (E) According to Erik Erikson, young adults are in the intimacy versus isolation stage. If, as an adolescent, you successfully found your own identity you will be ready to find intimacy with a partner by your early twenties. Young adulthood is a time for finding love and a meaningful relationship.

351. (B) The correct pairing in terms of age is choice (B). With all three, an individual is at age 50 or older. The other choices do not correctly correspond with age.

352. (E) Although some students might be tempted to choose (D), latency, the correct answer is genital. The genital stage begins at puberty and goes throughout adulthood. Adolescents would fall under that psychosexual stage.

353. (C) Robert Havighurst, David Elkind, and James Marcia all focused their work on adolescents. Freud, Gilligan, Kohlberg, and Piaget touched on, but did not focus their work on, adolescents.

354. (D) Children begin elementary school during the industry versus inferiority stage. Choice (C) might look tempting, but children in that stage are not quite old enough to be in elementary school.

355. (A) Robert Havighurst believed that all teenagers must complete a series of tasks before ending adolescence and beginning adulthood. Although many might seem outdated in today's world, they do include finding a partner, choosing a career path, and so on.

Chapter 18: Developmental Psychology: Death and Dying

356. (B) According to Erik Erikson, a person in late adulthood (65 and older) is in the integrity versus despair stage of his or her life. It is in this stage that people reflect and review their lives and the choices they made. On the positive side of this stage, if they look back and feel content with their friends and family and how they lived, they feel a sense of satisfaction or integrity.

357. (A) According to Elisabeth Kubler-Ross, people go through five stages when dealing with death and grief. Denial is first; anger comes second; bargaining, usually with a higher power, comes third; depression is fourth, and, finally, the last stage is acceptance. Although there are variations to this theory, for the purposes of the AP exam this is the order to know.

358. (C) Elisabeth Kubler-Ross formulated a stage theory on death and dying.

359. (B) In late adulthood, individuals experience a decline in perceptual speed, reaction time, and processing speed, all of which fall under cognitive abilities. Choice (D) might look enticing, but there is no evidence that people necessarily lose their intellectual ability as they age.

360. (D) According to Erik Erikson, an 80-year-old individual is in the integrity versus despair stage. If a person reflects back on his or her life and sees a series of crises, problems, and bad experiences, he or she will have feelings of regret or despair.

Chapter 19: Freudian Psychology

361. (A) Freud believed in the importance of the unconscious and that the forces of the unconscious originated in early childhood. Although Freud did study the conscious thought process, most of his work focused on the unconscious. He did not discuss the nature-nurture debate because he believed our personality stems from our environment. This would rule out choices (C) and (D).

362. (C) Freud believed the unconscious motivation explained why we say or do things we can't understand. Unconscious forces represent wishes, desires, or thoughts that, because of disturbing content, we automatically repress.

363. (B) Free association is one of Freud's important discoveries, which is still used today to help reveal a client's unconscious thought process. Choices (A), (C), and (D) can be eliminated because they are not real terms. Choice (E) represents the entire field of Freudian psychology.

364. (C) The id is Freud's first division of the mind. It contains two drives, sex and aggression. Sex and aggression are the source of all mental energy, according to Freud. The ego works to find acceptable ways of satisfying the id's desires. The superego's goal is applying moral values to individual desires.

365. (A) Unlike the ego and id, the superego focuses on the moral values and standards set by one's family, caregivers, and society. Because of this, children learn they must follow rules and regulations.

366. (C) Unlike the id and superego, the ego works as the negotiator between the other two. The ego follows the reality principle, which is the policy of satisfying desires only if they are socially acceptable.

367. (D) The pleasure principle acts to satisfy wishes or desires and avoid pain while ignoring social regulations. In the case of choice (D), the child acts out because his own wish was not met. The other choices do not show an individual avoiding pain and ignoring society's regulations.

368. (B) Choice (B) is the definition of a defense mechanism. Choices (A), (C), (D), and (E) are all examples of possible defense mechanisms; they do not actually define the term.

369. (E) Sublimation involves redirecting a threatening or forbidden desire, usually sexual, into a socially acceptable one. In this case, Todd puts his sexual frustration into a kickboxing class.

370. (A) Rationalization is the making up of acceptable excuses for behaviors that cause a person to feel anxious. In this case, Jay felt anxious about failing his class and, to reduce his anxiety, made the excuse that his teacher did not like him.

371. (E) Reaction formation involves turning unacceptable wishes into acceptable behaviors. In this case, the fact that Tom is still in love with the woman who broke up with him is an unacceptable behavior. Therefore he changes his desires into acceptable behavior.

372. (C) According to Freud, the preconscious is the part of the mind that exists right below the surface. It is the connection between the conscious and the unconscious.

373. (D) The phallic stage lasts from about three to six years of age. According to Freud it is a time when children's pleasure seeking is centered on the genitals. This stage is important for personality development because it is a time when boys discover their penis as a source of pleasure. According to Freud boys develop a sexual attraction to their mother and as a result feel jealousy toward their father. This concept became known as the Oedipus complex.

374. (D) The Electra complex was named for Electra, a woman in Greek mythology who killed her mother. Freud theorized that when girls discover they do not have a penis they turn against their mothers and develop sexual desires for their fathers.

375. (E) According to Freud, if a person becomes fixated during the phallic stage he or she may repress sexual urges later in life. Choices (A) and (D) could look like the correct answer, but sexual repression, according to Freud, comes from a fixation during the stage in which children become aware of pleasure from their genitals. During latency all sexual desires are repressed. The genital stage occurs after sexual repression would begin.

376. (A) Many psychologists, including neo-Freudians, did criticize Freud for placing too much emphasis on sexual conflict and the unconscious, and ignoring personal responsibility.

377. (C) The Oedipus complex is a process in which a child competes with the parent of the same sex for the affections and pleasures of the parent of the opposite sex.

378. (B) The id is pleasure seeking, and the superego is highly judgmental. The individual must listen to one of them. Choice (C) could look like the correct answer but because part of Grace's thought process is to keep the money, that is the pleasure-seeking id at work.

379. (E) According to Freud, when a person is fixated in the oral stage, later in life he or she may exhibit behavioral patterns that include choices (A), (B), (C), and (D).

380. (C) According to Freud, men who are fixated in the phallic stage cannot develop the proper relationship with their mother. This could lead to misogynistic behavior later in life.

Chapter 20: Personality Psychology

381. (A) Archetypes, according to Carl Jung, are universal themes that are part of the collective unconscious. These universal themes are terms or ideas shared by all cultures. Anima, feminine traits; animus, masculine traits; persona, the part of your personality you share publicly; and shadow, the part of your personality you do not publicly share, are all examples of archetypes.

382. (B) The humanistic approach to psychology is concerned with individual potential for growth and the unique perceptions that an individual has in terms of attaining that potential. Humanists believe all humans are born with a need for unconditional positive regard, acceptance, and love from others and themselves in order to achieve their full potential. Psychoanalysis focuses on childhood memories. Cognitive psychology focuses on changing one's thought process. Behavioral psychology focuses on changing one's behavior, and developmental psychology focuses on change versus stagnation.

383. (D) By taking the first letter of each trait, the "Big Five" traits make up the word OCEAN.

384. (B) Generally, type A personality people have more stressful lifestyles. Their fast-paced lifestyle leaves little time for relaxation. Type A personality individuals tend to be in professions that also increase their stress levels. They tend to be perfectionists and will not settle for less. All of these characteristics lead to an increase in potential for cardiac health problems.

385. (C) Carl Jung believed in the archetype called the persona. The persona is the universally shared understanding that people try to bring the best part of their personality to the forefront when in public view. They tend to hide the parts of their personality that they are not comfortable with. In this scenario, George allows the public (his classmates) to see his confidence while hiding his insecurities.

386. (D) The TAT, Thematic Apperception Test, is a projective test in which the subjects are given ambiguous pictures to tell a story about. The MMPI is a test that looks for personality abnormalities. The Rorschach test is an inkblot test. The LSAT is an exam students take to get into law school.

387. (E) Carl Rogers's self theory emphasizes unconditional positive regard for any true, authentic relationship to work. The self theory also places emphasis on congruency, which is when a person's true self, ideal self, and self-image are all congruent with each other. Self-actualization is the ability to reach one's full potential. Empathic understanding is truly understanding and listening to the needs of others. *Extraversion* is the only term that is not part of the self theory.

388. (B) Carl Rogers said that the self is made up of many self-perceptions and personality characteristics. The ideal self is the person whom an individual strives to become, and the real self is the person an individual actually is. These two personas should be consistent with one another.

389. (C) Choice (C) best describes self-efficacy. Many students might get confused with choice (E), but (E) actually defines the term *locus of control.* This term focuses more on whether fate or external causes contribute to our accomplishments.

390. (D) Motivation and determination are examples of internal causes of success. External causes would be putting things in the hands of chance or fate.

391. (D) Source traits are used to describe the 35 basic traits from Raymond Cattell's personality theory.

392. (B) The trait theory is an approach for analyzing personality structure. It identifies and classifies similarities and differences in personality characteristics. Factor analysis is an actual statistical method to find relationships among different items. Choice (A) can be eliminated because of the use of the word *genetics*. Choice (D) is too vague to be the correct answer. Choice (E) can be eliminated because of the use of the word *behaviors*.

393. (E) The Minnesota Multiphasic Personality Inventory (MMPI) is a true-false questionnaire. The Thematic Apperception Test is a writing test based on ambiguous pictures. The Rorschach test is an inkblot test. Although MMPI is a specific type of objective personality test, choice (D), that is not the best answer.

394. (A) Choice (A) is the only correct answer because it completely negates psychoanalysis and the unconscious by claiming that individuals have free will to reach their full potential.

395. (C) Choice (C) is the definition of archetypes.

396. (D) In contrast to Freud's belief in biological drives, Adler proposed that humans are motivated by social urges and feelings of inferiority. Choice (B) falls under Karen Horney. Choice (C) falls under Carl Rogers. Choice (E) is a learning behavior tool.

397. (B) Karen Horney believed that a major influence on personality development stemmed from the relationship a child had with his or her parents. Unlike Freud's belief in psychosexual conflict, Horney believed these conflicts are avoidable if children are raised in a loving and trusting environment.

398. (A) Part of Alfred Adler's theory focuses on the belief that people want to believe in simplistic proverbs, such as "treat people the way you want to be treated." As children, believing in these statements helps individuals cope with the complexities of reality.

399. (D) One major criticism neo-Freudians had regarding Freud was the emphasis he placed on sexual drives and conflicts in determining our behavior. Neo-Freudians believed much more strongly in our free will to make our own choices.

400. (D) This question clearly defines the humanistic approach.

Chapter 21: Stress and Coping

401. (B) Choice (B) is the definition of the term *stress*. The other choices are all examples of stress but do not give the actual definition.

402. (C) A threat appraisal is when the harm or loss has not yet occurred but the individual knows it will happen in the future. Choice (A) occurs when an individual has already sustained some damage or injury. Choice (B) occurs when there is potential for gain or personal growth but it is necessary to mobilize resources in order to achieve success.

403. (A) The fight-flight response directs a great amount of energy to the muscles and brain, therefore eliminating choice (B). Threatening physical stimuli trigger the fight-flight response. Choice (C) is incorrect because it does not solely calm the body down. Choice (D) is incorrect because the fight-flight sequence stimulates the pituitary gland, not the thyroid gland. Choice (E) is incorrect because the heart rate is increased first by the fight-flight sequence.

404. (D) This answer defines the term *psychosomatic symptoms.*

405. (B) The hypothalamus is stimulated when an individual appraises a situation as threatening, psychologically or physically. In turn, the hypothalamus triggers the pituitary gland and simultaneously activates the sympathetic nervous system.

406. (A) The adrenal medulla is activated by the sympathetic nervous system. Epinephrine, also known as adrenaline, is released. This hormone increases heart rate, blood pressure, blood flow to muscles, and release of blood sugar. The liver releases glycogen. Acetylcholine is released in both the PNS and CNS, not the adrenal medulla. Serotonin is primarily found in the gastrointestinal tract and the CNS. Dopamine is partially secreted by the hypothalamus, not the adrenal medulla.

407. (D) Hans Selye called his theory the general adaptation syndrome. This theory describes the body's reaction to stressful situations. The alarm stage is the initial reaction to stress. The resistance stage is the body's reaction to continued stress. The exhaustion stage is the body's reaction to continuous and long-term stress.

408. (A) Frustration is defined as the feeling that results when a person's attempt to reach a goal is blocked. In this scenario, the coach's goal of winning the game was blocked, causing frustration to occur. Choices (B), (D), and (E) could be examples of aggression but not necessarily frustration.

409. (E) Choices (B), (C), and (D) are all examples of three different interpretations of a primary appraisal.

410. (C) A challenge appraisal is based on one's potential for future success when the proper tools are used. In the example, Eva's professor is letting her know the importance of her success on the tests and quizzes. In other words, the professor is challenging her to do well on them.

411. (B) A harm/loss appraisal implies that an individual has already sustained some injury. A harm/loss appraisal elicits negative emotions such as fear and anxiety, and the individual feels stressed. The more negative emotions, the more stress the individual will have. Choice (D) could seem like the correct answer, but all primary appraisals elicit physiological arousal.

412. (C) During the exhaustion stage, extended periods of stress cause the body to become physically exhausted. Because the body is not meant to handle such strenuous work from the autonomic nervous system, the immune system weakens and there is a breakdown of the internal organs.

413. (A) The alarm stage is the initial reaction to stress. This is when the fight-flight response is activated. In this case, Charlene is entering the initial alarm stage just before the chorus concert starts.

414. (E) Choices (A), (B), (C), and (D) are all examples of the most common triggers of stress. Although fear can cause stress, it is not the major cause of stress for most people.

415. (D) Richard Lazarus's theory emphasized the importance of appraising a situation before experiencing stress.

Chapter 22: Disorders

416. (B) Choice (B) defines the term *mental disorder*. Choice (A) describes insanity. Choice (C) could be any number of types of mental disorders. Choice (D) is not the case for many disorders. Choice (E) is also not the case for all mental disorders.

417. (C) Insanity is legally defined as not knowing right from wrong.

418. (A) The key words from choice (A) associated with the learning perspective are *reinforcement* and *learned behavior*. The learning perspective theorizes that mental disorders are caused from the reinforcement of inappropriate behaviors. Choice (B) would be part of the cognitive perspective. Choice (C) would be part of the psychoanalytic perspective.

419. (C) The Diagnostic Statistical Manual lists common symptoms of psychological disorders. Professionals who classify and diagnose mental disorders use this manual. It does not list the causes of mental disorders, nor does it discuss the treatments.

420. (D) A somatoform disorder is marked by significant bodily symptoms with no physical causes. Although choice (C) might look tempting, individuals with a somatoform disorder do not make up their symptoms. Even though there is no physical cause for their symptoms, they are felt.

421. (E) Obsessive-compulsive disorder consists of persistent obsessive thoughts and irresistible impulses to perform some senseless behavior or ritual. This definition describes the scenario in choice (E).

422. (A) A conversion disorder refers to changing anxiety or emotional stress into real physical or neurological symptoms. In this scenario the soldier turned the psychological horrors of war into a physical symptom of blindness to protect himself.

423. (C) Hypochondriasis is actually classified as a somatoform disorder because of the physical symptoms with no physical cause. Therefore a hypochondriac is not suffering from an anxiety disorder.

424. (B) Generalized anxiety disorder is characterized by excessive worry about almost everything. These anxious feelings can cause irritability and difficulty concentrating.

425. (B) A panic disorder is characterized by unexpected panic attacks. When an individual is having a panic attack he or she has symptoms similar to those Fran showed.

426. (D) Agoraphobia is characterized by anxiety about being in places or situations in which there is no way to escape or the escape might be embarrassing. In many instances the fear causes people to never leave their home for years.

427. (D) Obsessive-compulsive disorder consists of obsessive, irrational thoughts, impulsive behavior, uncontrollable images, and ritualized behavior. Severe depression is not a symptom of the disorder.

428. (A) A conversion disorder is caused by emotional stress, which turns into physical symptoms with no cause.

429. (B) Axis II of the DSM-IV refers to disorders that involve patterns of personality traits that are maladaptive and involve impaired functioning.

430. (D) Recurring, multiple bodily symptoms with no physical cause mark somatoform disorders.

431. (A) Researchers interviewed more than 8,000 individuals between the ages of 15 and 54 years. Almost 50 percent reported having a substance abuse problem at some point in their life. To the surprise of many, substance abuse is considered to be a mental disorder.

432. (C) Exposure therapy gradually exposes the person to the real anxiety-provoking situation or objects that he or she is attempting to avoid by using ritualized behavior and obsessive thoughts.

433. (A) Axis I of the DSM-IV lists the symptoms and the duration of these symptoms for various mental disorders.

434. (C) Diathesis is a biological predisposition to the disorder. Choice (D) might look tempting, but the biochemical model states that mental disorders have a genetic component. This question places emphasis on the biological predisposition coming to the surface when a stressful event occurs.

435. (D) Gender-identity disorders involve the desire to become a member of the other sex.

Chapter 23: Mood Disorders and Schizophrenia

436. (E) Schizophrenia is not a mood disorder. A mood disorder is characterized as a prolonged and disturbed emotional state that affects an individual's thoughts and behaviors. Schizophrenia is a serious mental disorder with symptoms such as delusions and hallucinations.

437. (C) Dysthymic disorder is characterized by being chronically depressed for a period of two years.

438. (D) There is a direct link between levels of serotonin in the body and the onset of depression.

439. (A) Choice (A), major depression, is the only choice that is not a characteristic of a personality disorder. Major depression fits under mood disorders.

440. (B) This scenario describes a psychopath. Disregard for others, random violence, continuous lying, and little remorse are all symptoms of being a psychopath.

441. (C) Schizoid personality disorder is marked with discomfort in close relationships and distorted thinking. People suffering with dependent personality disorder have issues with codependency. People with paranoid personality disorder have patterns of distrust and suspicious thoughts about others. Antisocial personality disorder refers to patterns of disregarding the rights of others with no guilt or remorse.

442. (E) Individuals with paranoid personality disorder suffer from distrust and suspicion of others. They tend to assume that other people have evil tendencies or motives.

443. (B) Dissociative identity disorder is the presence of two or more identities or personality states. Each one has its own thought process and relation to the world. Much research has been done regarding DID. One explanation is a severe trauma from childhood, specifically abuse, which causes the mental split or dissociation of identities as a way of defending or coping with the memories of the trauma.

444. (A) The major indicator that Scott is suffering from antisocial personality disorder is the lack of remorse for his poor behavior.

445. (D) Unlike major depression or dysthymic disorder, individuals with bipolar disorder will go through several days or weeks with depression and then become manic. In this scenario, Pricilla shows her manic behavior by taking her life savings to spend on a shopping spree in Europe.

446. (B) The dopamine theory of schizophrenia says that the level of the neurotransmitter dopamine is overactive in schizophrenic patients, causing a wide range of symptoms. On the other hand, people who suffer from Parkinson's disease actually have low levels of the neurotransmitter dopamine.

447. (D) Manic behavior is not a symptom of schizophrenia. The other choices are all commonly seen symptoms of schizophrenia.

448. (E) Catatonic schizophrenia is characterized by periods of wild excitement or periods of rigid prolonged immobility. The person can remain in the same frozen posture for hours on end. Paranoid schizophrenia is characterized by hallucinations and delusions. Disorganized schizophrenia is marked by bizarre ideas and confused speech.

449. (A) Type I schizophrenia includes having positive symptoms, such as hallucinations, which is a distortion of normal functioning. The other choices are all examples of negative emotion, which means the sympathetic nervous system slows down.

450. (D) Researchers have had a hard time finding a single brain structure responsible for all of the symptoms seen in patients with schizophrenia. Recent studies have shown that schizophrenic brains tend to have an abnormally smaller thalamus.

451. (B) Dissociative fugue is marked by a sudden inability to recall one's own past. The person may not remember his or her identity. Choice (A) might look like a tempting answer, but dissociative amnesia is usually associated with a stressful or traumatic event, physically or psychologically. Choice (C), dissociative identity disorder, is also known as multiple personality disorder, which has nothing to do with memory loss.

452. (E) When testing a genetic marker or a genetic link, researchers must use identical twins because they share 100 percent of the same genetic makeup.

453. (B) Major depression is linked to below-normal levels of serotonin. Although there is evidence that below-normal dopamine levels also affect depression, choice (A) says moderate levels, not below-normal levels.

454. (A) Developmental disorders are first diagnosed in early childhood or adolescence. Autism falls under this label because its diagnosis is made in early childhood.

455. (D) Narcissists absolutely suffer from an inflated sense of self. Some students might want to put choice (A) as the answer, but that is not necessarily true for narcissists, more so for individuals suffering with borderline personality disorder.

Chapter 24: Therapies

456. (C) This question uses the term *past experiences*, which corresponds directly to psychoanalytic therapy and past conflict.

457. (B) Insight therapy focuses on identifying the causes of the client's problems. Once the client has an insight into the cause of the problem, possible solutions are discussed.

458. (A) Unlike a clinical psychologist, a psychiatrist is a medical doctor and can therefore prescribe medication using biomedical treatment.

459. (D) Because ECT can be quick and effective, it works for clients who could possibly be suicidal.

460. (E) Client-centered therapy helps the client assume a self-actualizing state. This therapy empowers the client to reach his or her full potential. With the use of positive regard, the client feels encouraged to take charge of the therapy session.

461. (A) Prozac is part of a category of drugs that work as selective serotonin reuptake inhibitors. In other words, serotonin becomes more available in the body, helping those who suffer from depression.

462. (C) Rational emotive therapy (RET) is a cognitive therapy that focuses on reconstructing the client's self-defeating ways of thinking.

463. **(B)** Choice (B) is the definition of aversive therapy. Aversive therapy basically uses a stimulus-response approach to rid an individual of negative behavior.

464. **(D)** Most people associate dream analysis with psychoanalysis. Gestalt therapy also includes dream analysis, which helps to look at the whole picture of an individual's conflict.

465. **(A)** Transference is a Freudian belief that describes a client-therapist relationship. In this process the client transfers emotions and substitutes the therapist for someone important in the client's life.

466. **(A)** Cognitive therapy, as developed by Aaron Beck, assumes that we have automatic negative thoughts that we continually say to ourselves. By using these thoughts we actually distort our perception of the world.

467. **(B)** Systematic desensitization is a behavioral technique that gradually exposes a client to a specific feared object while simultaneously practicing relaxation techniques.

468. **(D)** The humanist approach is built on the importance of empathy and support. Behavioral therapies are sometimes criticized for being too mechanical. The humanist approach focuses most on unconditional positive regard.

469. **(C)** Rational emotive therapy, according to Albert Ellis, works to rid the client of negative thoughts, which are impeding his or her achievement of life goals.

470. **(A)** Free association is a technique that encourages the client to talk about any thoughts or images that enter his or her head. This free-flowing talk is supposed to provide material from the unconscious.

471. **(E)** The presence of the disorder is correlated with reduced levels of light, which accompanies the onset of winter. Controlled exposure to artificial light is often successful in treating seasonal affective disorder.

472. **(A)** Self-actualization is associated with the humanistic approach, not psychoanalysis.

473. **(A)** Aaron Beck developed a kind of cognitive therapy that specifically focused on ridding individuals of the negative thoughts that prevent them from achieving their goals.

474. **(D)** This statement specifically defines the term *biofeedback*. The key word that can help an individual answer this question correctly is *feedback*. Feedback refers to an individual, in this case the client, receiving immediate information.

475. **(C)** Behavioral therapy is used in treating anxiety disorders through systematic desensitization therapy. Behavioral therapy is used to help individuals with autism through positive reinforcement. Behavioral therapists work with drug addicts to try to find what triggers their addictive tendencies.

Chapter 25: Social Psychology

476. (C) Researchers have analyzed group decision-making processes involved in making bad decisions, such as the Bay of Pigs. They discovered something called "groupthink." This occurs when group discussions emphasize sticking together to make the "best" decision. There is usually one member who discourages ideas that might threaten group unity. In the Bay of Pigs situation, many of John F. Kennedy's advisors did just that.

477. (A) Asch's classic experiment on group conformity had individuals conforming on something as simple as two lines being the same length. In this case, social pressures influence conformity. Many students might get confused with obedience, but that was actually Milgram's experiment.

478. (B) Self-serving bias refers to explaining our successes by attributing them to our dispositions or personality traits and attributing our failures to the situation.

479. (A) Philip Zimbardo's "mock prison" experiment in the early 1970s is extremely important to know for the AP exam. He was interested in studying group dynamics in prison. He got student volunteers to play the roles of prisoners and prison guards. The volunteers became immersed in their roles, and many of the guards conformed so much to what was expected of their role that they began to punish and humiliate the volunteers who played the roles of powerless inmates.

480. (D) Choice (D) basically defines the term *cognitive dissonance*. Essentially, we strive to keep our behaviors and attitudes consistent with one another. Leon Festinger coined this term to describe the internal tension when our behavior and attitude do not mesh.

481. (B) Foot in door is a method of persuasion that relies on compliance to a second request if a person complies with a small request first. Students might confuse the correct answer for door in face, but that is actually the complete opposite. With door in face, an individual will settle for a small request after rejecting a larger one.

482. (C) Stanley Milgram originally developed this experiment to try to better understand the answer many Nazi soldiers gave in the Nuremberg trials. Milgram's experiment deals specifically with obedience to authority figures.

483. (A) Milgram discovered that people were less likely to be obedient if the authority figure was in another room. People were more likely to be obedient when the authority figure was standing in the room with them.

484. (D) The diffusion of responsibility theory says that in the presence of others, individuals feel less personal responsibility and are less likely to take action in a situation where help is required.

485. (B) The fundamental attribution error refers to our tendency, when looking for a cause of a person's behavior, to focus on the person's disposition and ignore or overlook the situational reasons.

486. (E) Part of Asch's results showed that individuals are less likely to conform in certain situations; one is if there is just one other person who does not conform in the group.

487. (C) Group cohesion is simply group togetherness, which is determined by how much group members perceive that they share common attributes, goals, and values.

488. (B) In the Lapierre experiment, Lapierre wrote letters to several hotel and restaurant owners during a time when many Asian Americans were discriminated against and asked them if they would allow Asians into their place of business. Most refused these potential customers. But, in person, those same restaurant and hotel owners invited these people in.

489. (C) Compliance is a kind of conformity in which we give in to social pressure in our public responses but do not change our private beliefs.

490. (D) Deindividuation states that we are more likely to behave out of character when there are high levels of anonymity and low probability of getting caught. Choice (E) might look correct, but that is actually an example of diffusion of responsibility.

491. (A) Using specific dilemmas, researchers compared the recommendations from individuals in a group with those made by the group after it had engaged in discussion. Group discussions change individuals' judgments, such as when groups urge a more risky recommendation than do individuals.

492. (B) Groupthink occurs when group discussions emphasize sticking together with an agreement over the use of critical thinking. This situation creates an "in group" and an "out group." Allowing all group members the freedom to share their opinions can eliminate groupthink.

493. (D) In this scenario, Randy believes he personally works harder than others, attributing his success to his own disposition. While choice (E) might look enticing, just because Rebi overestimates her ability to run a program does not mean she is attributing her success to her own disposition.

494. (A) A self-fulfilling prophecy is a situation in which a person has a strong belief about a future behavior and then acts unknowingly to fulfill or carry out that behavior. In this case, Jean believed her professor so much that her behavior reflected the statement.

495. (B) Because the question asked what the dissonance theory would state, David would have to change one of his beliefs in order to reduce his cognitive inconsistencies.

496. (B) Although choice (D) might look like the correct answer, it is not specific enough to this scenario. The actor-observer bias occurs when a person judges other people's behavior based on their personal attributes and the person's own behavior based on the situation.

497. (B) Although many people believe in the notion that opposites attract, the reality is that individuals tend to date and marry people similar to themselves in terms of morals, values, and life perspectives.

498. (D) The just-world hypothesis is the belief that good people do good things and bad people do bad things. To understand why an individual was raped, the just-world hypothesis would cause a person to assume the victim "asked for it."

499. (E) This scenario defines the concept of social facilitation, which is the increase in performance in the presence of a crowd.

500. (C) Diffusion of responsibility is the idea that in the presence of others, individuals feel less personal responsibility and are less likely to take action in a situation where help is required.